W9-ANF-296

Discernment
& Decision Making
Are you making the right choice?

By SA SCOTT

Discernment & Decision Making
Are you making the right choice?

©2011 SA Scott / WordSmyth Publishing
www.cbcdundalk.org/wordsmythministries.php

For information regarding this book please contact Calvary Baptist Church of Dundalk, Maryland, or send an Email to: sascott@cbcdundalk.org

Cover Design: Hillary Grantham at dropsofdesign@yahoo.com Special thanks to Judy Rolfe for editing and proofing the manuscript. A special thanks to Pastor Giovanelli and Jimmy Ryder for encouraging me to print. A special thanks to Linda Milam of FBC Publications & Printing, for her technical help. Most of all I give very special thanks to my wife, Cecilia Scott, for encouraging me in my work for the Lord. She is a real blessing to me.

All definitions used in this book were taken from Webster's 1828 version of the dictionary. All Scripture was taken from the precious KING JAMES VERSION.

ISBN: 978-1-60208-289-2

Printed in the USA by
FBC Publications & Printing
3607 Oleander Ave.
Ft. Pierce, FL 34982.
www.fbcpublications.com

PREFACE

1 Kings 3: 5 "In Gibeon the LORD appeared to Solomon in a dream by night: and God said, Ask what I shall give thee. 6 And Solomon said, Thou hast shewed unto thy servant David my father great mercy, according as he walked before thee in truth, and in righteousness, and in uprightness of heart with thee; and thou hast kept for him this great kindness, that thou hast given him a son to sit on his throne, as it is this day. 7 And now, O LORD my God, thou hast made thy servant king instead of David my father: and I am but a little child: I know not how to go out or come in. 8 And thy servant is in the midst of thy people which thou hast chosen, a great people, that cannot be numbered nor counted for multitude. 9 Give therefore thy servant an understanding heart to judge thy people, that I may discern between good and bad: for who is able to judge this thy so great a people? 10 And the speech pleased the Lord, that Solomon had asked this thing. 11 And God said unto him, Because thou hast asked this thing, and hast not asked for thyself long life; neither hast asked riches for thyself, nor hast asked the life of thine enemies; but hast asked for thyself understanding to discern judgment; 12 Behold, I have done according to thy words: lo, I have given thee a wise and an understanding heart; so that there was none like thee before thee, neither after thee shall any arise like unto thee. 13 And I have also given thee that which thou hast not asked, both riches, and honour: so that there shall not be any among the kings like unto thee all thy days. 14 And if

thou wilt walk in my ways, to keep my statutes and my commandments, as thy father David did walk, then I will lengthen thy days. 15 And Solomon awoke; and, behold, it was a dream. And he came to Jerusalem, and stood before the ark of the covenant of the LORD, and offered up burnt offerings, and offered peace offerings, and made a feast to all his servants. 16 Then came there two women, that were harlots, unto the king, and stood before him."

Discernment & Decision Making

Table of contents

Discernment & Decision Making

Discernment & Decision Making

INTRODUCTION

Life is filled with decision making. We will make thousands of decisions throughout the course of our life. We make many decisions which we consider as small decisions. Yet we must remember that with every decision we make there will be consequence or fruit.

Some decisions seem so easy to make, and yet they are filled with subtle and unseen dangers. There are decisions we fail to make, and then others we make which later we discover should never have been made. There is the issue of timing and maintenance in decision making. There are many aspects to decision making and keeping.

How are we to learn to make good decisions in life?

When I was a pastor, I started a class for the college and career age group. God had brought it to my attention that they were the group for me to teach because they were at the crossroads of living. Hence we called it the "Crossroads Class." They had many decisions to make that would impact the rest of their life for good or for bad. They needed the Alpha and Omega eyes of God to guide them. They needed to know the will of God. They needed to learn how to make decisions. So I began to take them to the Word of God to find out how to make decisions. I told them to study His Word to find His will.

We learned so much together. I decided that the entire church needed to learn how to discern the good from the bad and the right from the wrong. I embarked on a journey in study that took us 32 or 33 weeks to complete. However, I am not sure I ever finished the study. How important it is to know how to make a right decision, but more important than that, it is essential to do what we learn.

> Deuteronomy 30: 11 "For this commandment which I command thee this day, it is not hidden from thee, neither is it far off. 12 It is not in heaven, that thou shouldest say, Who shall go up for us to heaven, and bring it unto us, that we may hear it, and do it? 13 Neither is it beyond the sea, that thou shouldest say, Who shall go over the sea for us, and bring it unto us, that we may hear it, and do it? 14 But the word is very nigh unto thee, in thy mouth, and in thy heart, **that thou mayest do it**."

God has made right and wisdom obtainable.

"Written for our learning"

> Romans 15:4 "For whatsoever things were written aforetime were written for our learning, that we through patience and comfort of the scriptures might have hope."

> 1 Corinthians 10:11 "Now all these things happened unto them for ensamples: and they are written for our admonition, upon whom the ends of the world are come. 12 Wherefore let him that thinketh he standeth take heed lest he fall. 13 There hath no temptation taken you but such as is common to man: but God is faithful, who will not suffer you to be tempted above that ye are able; but will with the temptation also make a way to escape, that ye may be able to bear it."

Discernment & Decision Making

2 Timothy 3:16 "All scripture is given by inspiration of God, and is profitable for doctrine, for reproof, for correction, for instruction in righteousness: 17 That the man of God may be perfect, throughly furnished unto all good works."

God has given us a check and balance system that we may have confidence and peace in our decision making. If we want to know what is right to do, we can find out. We can find example after ensample, or patterns and models of right and wrong decisions, contained within the Word of God.

The Bible has many examples of principles to live by and the effects from not listening to the wisdom, Word, and counsel of God. Therefore, when learning or studying discernment and decision making, we must take time to look at several stories in the Bible and see where they went wrong. It is important for us to learn, or to critique these stories, but we must avoid any urge to be critical of the people in these stories.

We must take note of those who have made bad decisions; for there are many good godly men down through the ages that have made very bad decisions, which carried long term effects, affecting other lives besides their own. So it could surely happen to us.

We must study and learn from the characters of the Bible in the spirit and attitude of Galatians 6:1 which says, "Brethren, if a man be overtaken in a fault, ye which are spiritual, restore such an one in the spirit of meekness; considering thyself, lest thou also be tempted."

I also want to stress or emphasize one last point before we look at some Biblical examples of bad decision making. When they did right and made good decisions, it is because they trusted God more than themselves. Time after time, in the examples we can find in the lives of those we see in the Word of God, their BIGGEST problem is because they leaned to their own understanding. **It is the common denominator**.

Proverbs 3: 5 "Trust in the LORD with all thine heart; and lean not unto thine own understanding. 6 In all thy ways acknowledge him, and he shall direct thy paths. 7 Be not wise in thine own eyes: fear the LORD, and depart from evil. 8 It shall be health to thy navel, and marrow to thy bones."

Psalms 1:1 "Blessed *is* the man that walketh not in the counsel of the ungodly, nor standeth in the way of sinners, nor sitteth in the seat of the scornful. 2 But his delight *is* in the law of the LORD; and in his law doth he meditate day and night. 3 And he shall be like a tree planted by the rivers of water, that bringeth forth his fruit in his season; his leaf also shall not wither; and whatsoever he doeth shall prosper. 4 The ungodly *are* not so: but *are* like the chaff which the wind driveth away. 5 Therefore the ungodly shall not stand in the judgment, nor sinners in the congregation of the righteous. 6 For the LORD knoweth the way of the righteous: but the way of the ungodly shall perish."

CHAPTER ONE
Solomon asked for wisdom

1 Kings 3:5—15

We need the ability to discern or distinguish one thing from another; truth from falsehood, help from harm, the dangerous from the tame and virtue from vice. We can get this knowledge from God and His Word, and from the people He has given to help us. We can gain understanding from others or from personal experiences.

God is essential to decision making because He has the *alpha and omega eyes* that can see the beginning and end of all things. He is the One to go to for wisdom. We can go to His Word, and we can go to Him in prayer to ask guidance with **every** decision we encounter. It is the wisest way to live.

We need God's guidance whether we are at a certain crossroad, making life changing, path altering decisions, or as we go through the day. We need God's help to keep us from making bad decisions that can be very costly over time.

> ## It is my recommendation and practice that Proverbs be read and studied daily.

We will often be faced with new challenges and responsibilities whereby we will need the help of God. He is more than willing to help us know and understand the truth. He can help distinguish the dangerous from the tame.

Discernment & Decision Making

The truth is obtainable and within reach, **if** we truly seek to know it [Deuteronomy 30:11—14]

God has given us access to truth so that we can find it, obtain it, and daily live it. You don't have to be a Bible scholar to have wisdom for good decision making. God has graciously made wisdom available for those who ask.

James 1:5 "If any of you lack wisdom, let him ask of God, that giveth to all *men* liberally, and upbraideth not; and it shall be given him."

Most people do not go to the source of all wisdom when making a decision, but base their decisions on feelings and emotions. Their decision making is based on how they will personally benefit. Hence, God, the Bible, truth, and righteousness are lost in self preservation when one only seeks to please themselves.

Many times people make decisions with a loose understanding of God's word, or without appreciation or consideration for the will of God. His perspective is not even considered, as though God has no interest in the outcome of His own children.

What hurt will follow foolish and unlearned decisions?

It is God's intention to give experienced counselors into every life. We have fathers, husbands, pastors, mothers, guidance counselors at schools, teachers, bosses, as well as others who have been given to help us make decisions. That does not mean that all people in your life will give you good counsel or advice. Some will be experienced in one area of your life but not in another.

Discernment & Decision Making

I personally have three levels of friendships or acquaintances with whom I communicate. I have those I help and mentor. Then I have those who are my peers or acquaintances. I also have those whom I go to, to check my thinking or to sharpen me. They can help mentor or guide me as needed.

It seems healthy for me to have each of these levels in my life. Some are inlets and some outlets. However, we must be careful to use each for the purpose in which they are intended. My peers are not necessarily those I would go to for deep counsel. I can utilize them as a sounding board to bounce ideas off of, now and again, but I do not counsel with them about the deeper things or when I am perplexed and need my thinking challenged. I am not going to ask someone I am mentoring, for advice, as it will change the dynamic of the relationship. I have given counsel to those who did not realize it at the time, and I have received counsel which I did not realize until later.

I want to point out some things surrounding this issue of discernment, decision making, counsel and counselors as a foundation. It is important for us to understand why God gave us counselors. They are no threat to you *if* the truth is what you seek. It is a wise thing to seek *right* counsel from the *right* kind of people. Right counsel for one person might not be a right counselor for me. God will help manage our counselor, if we let Him. He will give favor to the counsel and to the one receiving counsel. It will be a divine match. No matter how many people come to you for counsel or wisdom, there are times when it will be good to have your thinking challenged by a wise counselor. Solomon could have used good counsel before he started his process of falling.

Proverbs 11:14 "Where no counsel *is*, the people fall: but in the multitude of counsellors *there is* safety."

Proverbs 15:22 "Without counsel purposes are disappointed: but in the multitude of counsellors they are established."

Proverbs 24:6 "For by wise counsel thou shalt make thy war: and in multitude of counsellors *there is* safety."

People fail, or fall, where there is no wise counsel. Disappointment will come when there is no counsel. Wise counsel can be of great service to you when there is much at stake. A leader might be a wise man, but he will best show his wisdom by never making a major decision without going to trustworthy counselors to ask their advice before he determines the direction he should go. He will start and finish such an inquisition with God.

There are 'how to' patterns and principles in the Word of God, which we can go to for whatever question we have, to find a solution to whatever we need. For instances, the book of Proverbs is filled with them. It is my recommendation and practice that Proverbs be read and studied daily. It will help to condition our thinking.

We must be in the habit of reading and studying the Word of God, every day. We must memorize and meditate upon it daily. This will keep it fresh in our heart and mind. Then we should be with God in prayer throughout the day. As we maintain these practices we can stay fresh with wisdom. That way, when it is decision time, we will work cautiously to seek the right answer. [James 1:21-25] As the word is engrafted in our life, we will be more aware of the weakness of our own understanding in the light of Scripture. The Word must be hid in our hearts so that it is present in time of need.

Solomon was wise enough to ask God for wisdom. He sought God for it. He believed that wisdom and discernment were more valuable than earthly treasures or protection from his enemies. He knew if he was to follow in his father's footsteps and lead God's people, he would need an abundance of wisdom.

We must always see our challenges or task as bigger than us. We must never think we have the answer in and of ourselves. We must not be so sure of ourselves that we fail to ask God. We must never forget the enemy would enjoy messing up the plan **we** put forth, just like he did at the battle of Ai. Seek God first, before everything you do.

Matthew 6:33 "But **seek ye first** the kingdom of God, and his righteousness; and all these things shall be added unto you."

Discernment & Decision Making

It would be good to get into the habit of asking God for wisdom, discernment, and understanding every day.

WISDOM, n. s as z. [G. See Wise.]

1. The right use or exercise of knowledge; the choice of laudable ends, and of the best means to accomplish them. This is wisdom in act, effect, or practice. If wisdom is to be considered as a faculty of the mind, it is the faculty of discerning or judging what is most just, proper and useful, and if it is to be considered as an acquirement, it is the knowledge and use of what is best, most just, most proper, most conducive to prosperity or happiness. Wisdom in the first sense, or practical wisdom, is nearly synonymous with discretion. I differs somewhat from prudence, in this respect; prudence is the exercise of sound judgment in avoiding evils; wisdom is the exercise of sound judgment either in avoiding evils or attempting good. Prudence then is a species, of which wisdom is the genus.

Wisdom gained by experience, is of inestimable value.

It is hoped that our rulers will act with dignity and wisdom; that they will yield everything to reason, and refuse everything to force.

Noah Webster's 1828 Dictionary

James 1:5 "If any of you lack wisdom, let him ask of God, that giveth to all *men* liberally, and upbraideth not; and it shall be given him."

CHAPTER TWO
Spiritual or Carnal?

Exodus 18:13—27

Moses was to stand in judgment before the people. When the burden of judging such a large group of people became too heavy, Moses enlisted the assistance of other spiritual men. They were to aid and assist him in judging matters of The Law. They would decide the small matters and bring the weightier issues to Moses.

Exodus 18:21 "Moreover thou shalt provide out of all the people able men, such as fear God, men of truth, hating covetousness; and place such over them, to be rulers of thousands, and rulers of hundreds, rulers of fifties, and rulers of tens:"

We can see in this passage the levels of decision making. The men that Moses recruited to stand and judge the people were men who were filled with wisdom and discernment. Therefore they were qualified to handle matters of judgment. They were given guidelines to follow. They could not be respecters of persons and when the problem they faced was too much for them, they had to see the issue as important and valuable enough to seek Moses' help to settle the dispute.

They needed to be Scripturally and spiritually-minded.

[1 Corinthians 2:1-16] 14 "But the natural man receiveth not the things of the Spirit of God: for they are foolishness unto him: neither can he know them, because they are spiritually discerned. 15 But he that is spiritual judgeth all things, yet he himself is judged of no man."

17

Discernment & Decision Making

We must be able to see everything on the spiritual plane. Everything we do has something to do with the spiritual; whether it is for good or bad. When we do things, or when things happen to us, do we discern the matter in light of the spiritual?

Decisions can make you or break you.

Many people have an inability to comprehend or understand spiritual things because they do not think spiritually, or scripturally. Whenever there is a lack of spiritual discernment in a person's life, it is most likely because of a lack of scriptural discipleship in their life. Their mind and their thinking have **not** been renewed [Romans 12:1, 2] by the Word of God.

We must realize that those who are not saved cannot judge spiritual matters [1Corinthians 6:1-8]. A person who does not understand the Bible and the principles of the Bible cannot properly judge spiritually [1Corinthians 2:14-16]. A person without spiritual discernment will not judge well in spiritual matters.

Discernment is not a spiritual gift, but for the Christian it is a learned discipline. A Christian with a spiritual understanding will take the eternal into account when making decisions. Hence the spiritual and the eternal will be relevant in all matters of everyday life. As we study God's Word "to show ourselves approved UNTO GOD", we put ourselves in position to have better discernment. This is very important because **decisions can make or break you**.

DISCERNMENT, n. The act of discerning; also, the power or faculty of the mind, by which it distinguishes one thing from another, as truth from

18

falsehood, virtue from vice; acuteness of judgment; power of perceiving differences of things or ideas, and their relations and tendencies. The errors of youth often proceed from the want of discernment.

Noah Webster's 1828 Dictionary

Like Solomon before us, we must ask God for wisdom and discernment so we are poised and prepared every moment for the decisions that will arise without warning. Whenever possible, we must put off making a decision so we have time to consider the matter in prayer. This will give God the opportunity to speak to us.

Not only must we be spiritually and Biblically minded to make good decisions, we should be aware of matters that are close to us. When a person is, or could be, a *respecter of persons,* or emotionally attached to the issue, they must be very careful in judgment and / or making decisions. It is best to get a second opinion when dealing with delicate and serious issues, just to check our thinking, especially when we are personally involved.

In addition, asking a saved person versus an unsaved person can make a difference in the response you get. Our counsel should come from a saved person whenever possible.

Leviticus 10:10-11; Ezekiel 22:26; Ezekiel 44:23

We must have a keen awareness of spiritual things so that we can and will be able to separate the holy from the profane. It is the idea, in short, of determining what is right over what is wrong. Many times there is more at stake than we realize. Someone in a position of leadership or experience can help us see things that we have missed, or because of the nature of the situation a person chooses to overlook.

The constitution of the United States has been trampled on and violated by judges who have catered to a personal agenda. They treat the constitution as a living document that can change with time. They have followed the migration in agenda or emphasis of our nation and in doing so they have misapplied the law. Instead of honoring the framework of the constitution, they over-judge or under-judge to satisfy some new national trend in ideology. More often personal feelings and social change have been factored into the process of judgment. Thereby judges have set presidents in law that have hurt the system of judgment overall. Unconstitutional judgment or decisions have had and will lead to more long-term catastrophic results. One bad decision can impact the moral direction of an entire nation. These profane decisions will get God's attention. Then God will answer with a counter-judgment of His own.

'Roe v. Wade' is now a classic case of a bad decision which has dire ongoing ramification. The life of the baby has been overlooked, set aside and denied, in order to give a woman the choice to keep or kill her baby. The quality of the woman's life is the main issue. The lifestyle of the woman has been determined more important than the life of a baby. Rarely is it a matter of a woman's life being at risk, but it is always a matter of a baby's life which is at stake.

> Legalized **abortion** spawned
> the slow death of a nation

Discernment & Decision Making

This is a doubled-minded issue. For instance, a drunk driver can run into a woman who is pregnant and kill the unborn child, even if the mother lives it is still considered 'vehicular homicide'. This exposes 'Roe vs. Wade' as a very wrong, bad, and unjust decision as it contradicts and corrupts the law and judgment. The **only** difference is that one momma wanted her baby, and the other did not.

If you are inclined to amen, don't say it too loudly; many Christians will pervert the laws and judgments of God when their life or the life of someone in their family will be affected by the decision that is made. At this point, I am not talking about 'Roe vs. Wade.'

Acts 10:34 "Then Peter opened *his* mouth, and said, Of a truth I perceive that God is no respecter of persons:"

When it comes to discernment and making decisions, we must be careful to be just and consistent. We must not be a 'respecter of persons,' especially when we are the person we respect the most.

Two things are necessary so that we can have discernment in our decision making. Number one, we must ask for wisdom. God has wisdom available, but we must diligently ask or seek Him for it. [Proverbs 8:32-35]

James 1:5 "If any of you lack wisdom, let him ask of God, that giveth to all *men* liberally, and upbraideth not; and it shall be given him."

John 11:22 "But I know, that even now, whatsoever thou wilt ask of God, God will give *it* thee."

We must ask God regularly for discernment in our decision making, and then we must respond properly to what God tells us to do. It does no good for us to ask God for His help and then fail to do what God has told us to do. Why ask if we are not going follow His Word and receive the help He offers? [Proverbs 1:1—33]

If we reject wisdom then we will suffer its absence.

Number two, it is very important for us to study and learn the Word of God. It is where we will find the living testimony of God's wisdom which has been given to man down through the ages.

2 Timothy 2:15 "**Study** to shew thyself approved unto God, a workman that needeth not to be ashamed, rightly dividing the word of truth."

Why should we study the Scriptures? So that we can know the Scripture and so the Scriptures can give light to guide our lives. We need the Bible to be our map book and compass for living.

Psalm 119:105 NUN. "Thy word *is* a lamp unto my feet, and a light unto my path."

Proverbs 6: 23 "For the commandment is a lamp; and the law is light; and reproofs of instruction are the way of life:"

The principles for living life are contained within the Word of God. They are available to give us knowledge and understanding so that we can make good decisions.

What is the difference in knowledge and understanding?

Discernment & Decision Making

KNOWL'EDGE, n. nol'lej. 1. A clear and certain perception of that which exists, or of truth and fact; the perception of the connection and agreement, or disagreement and repugnancy of our ideas. We can have no knowledge of that which does not exist. God has a perfect knowledge of all his works. Human knowledge is very limited, and is mostly gained by observation and experience.

2. Learning; illumination of mind.
3. Skill; as a knowledge of seamanship.
4. Acquaintance with any fact or person.
5. Cognizance; notice. Ruth 2.
6. Information; power of knowing.

UNDERSTAND'ING, ppr. 1. Comprehending; apprehending the ideas or sense of another, or of a writing; learning or being informed. 2. a. Knowing; skillful. He is an understanding man.

UNDERSTAND'ING, n. 1. The faculty of the human mind by which it apprehends the real state of things presented to it, or by which it receives or comprehends the ideas which others express and intend to communicate.

2. Knowledge; exact comprehension. Right understanding consists in the perception of the visible or probably agreement or disagreement of ideas.

Noah Webster's 1828 Dictionary

I can know a car exists in the parking lot and not understand how it works. I can have knowledge of the verses of the Scriptures and not understand the principles that are set forth in the Bible.

Discernment & Decision Making

Proverbs 4:7 "Wisdom *is* the principal thing; *therefore* get wisdom: and with all thy getting get understanding."

Luke 10:42 "But one thing is needful: and Mary hath chosen that good part, which shall not be taken away from her."

Mary sat at the feet of Jesus to learn from Him, and there was no greater thing she could do. If it was best for Mary then, it is great for us now.

The best way to get knowledge and understanding is to read and study the stories of the Bible. We will see good and bad decisions made by people in the Bible. We can study the short term and long term effects of their decisions. The Bible is the only book to see the entire story of people's lives, from a heavenly perspective, as they unfold. We know they are true, and we have the benefit of God narrating and explaining these stories. We can also gain wisdom by sitting under the preaching of God's Word to learn the percepts and principles contained within its pages. [Psalm 27:4; 26:8; 65:4]

Hebrews 13:17 "Obey them that have the rule over you, and submit yourselves: for they watch for your souls, as they that must give account, that they may do it with joy, and not with grief: for that *is* unprofitable for you." {have...: or, guide}

If you believe that God uses the Holy Spirit to communicate to a pastor and then uses that pastor or preacher [Ephesians 4:11, 12] to communicate wisdom unto you through the preaching of the Word of God, then it is very important to be in each and every corporate counseling session during every church service.

Discernment & Decision Making

1 Peter 5:2 "Feed the flock of God which is among you, taking the oversight *thereof*, not by constraint, but willingly; not for filthy lucre, but of a ready mind;"

We get wisdom for decision making by asking God for wisdom, by reading the Bible, by listening to preaching, and through godly counsel. This counseling will come by way of the spiritual leaders God will bring into our life, like a pastor, preacher, godly teacher, husband, as well as our father and mother. [Ephesians 4:11, 12]

Proverbs 11:14 "Where no counsel *is*, the people fall: but in the multitude of counsellors *there is* safety."

Proverbs 24:6 "For by wise counsel thou shalt make thy war: and in multitude of counsellors *there is* safety."

We must be spiritually and Biblically minded so we can and will make good decisions for our life and the life of those God has made our responsibility. Our mind will be equipped and renewed to think spiritually as we ask God for wisdom and as we allow ourselves to be influenced by reading, studying and listening to the Word of God. We must be people of prayer. We must learn to pray about every decision we make.

Discernment & Decision Making

NOTES TO LIVE BY: Note to self, ask GOD for wisdom and discernment every day.

CHAPTER THREE

The **very** costly decision of Adam and Eve

Genesis 2: 15—17; Genesis 3:1—7

Father knows best. When we come to the crossroads of any decision we face or will need to make, the first thing we must do is look to God. He does know best. We must have faith in the alpha / omega eyes of Almighty God. He is ever present, always knowing, and He lives in eternity past, present, and future. He is most qualified to guide and direct our life.

The next thing to consider or determine is whether the decision has already been made for us. I would tell you that God has given us a vast and all-encompassing manual for living. The Bible is designed to help guide us. There are many decisions we do not need to make. That is to say that the Word of God is given to make many of our decisions for us.

We should never stress about making **made** decisions.

When we study and consider the story of Adam and Eve, we find that God had already given instructions regarding the **forbidden** tree. There is no need to rename a tree that has a name. Do not rename a "forbidden" tree the bidden tree. Their first mistake was rejecting the Word of God and making a decision against a decision that was already made for them. There is no need to ponder for a solution regarding a decision that has been made for you.

Ephesians 4:27 "Neither give place to the devil."

Discernment & Decision Making

Next we find Eve listening to Satan. He is a very bad counselor for he has an agenda of his own. He appeared to work for them as he was working against them. She allowed him to influence her outside the bounds of where she should have sought counsel or taken advice. God's Word and her husband should have been her two authority-advisors in her life. They were available and sufficient for decision making. Be very careful not to take ungodly counsel, or counsel from those who do not have responsibility over your life.

[2 Corinthians 11:13—15] Satan will never appear to you in his *ugliest* form. I am not talking about horns and a pitch-fork. I am saying that he will come as a *helpful* angel of light while his true agenda is hidden. He talks or communicates today through a variety of ways. Many of his ways might seem credible. The question is whether it is a place where God said we should go to get our knowledge or direction. [1 Kings 13:1-24]

There are many avenues, vessels, and venues like music, movies, talk-radio, television, magazines, self-help books, secular colleges, universities, or a best friend, that are filled with gibberish which many will consider good counsel or believe contain good knowledge.

According to 2 Corinthians 11:13-15, Satan has his ministers of "light." He has his wolves which are nicely dressed in sheep's clothing to trick, confuse, and derail the Christian from the will of God. Satan might use a relative or a friend who seems to have the corner view on life itself. **Watch out! Satan likes to play dress-up!**

Matthew 7:15 "Beware of false prophets, which come to you in sheep's clothing, but inwardly they are ravening wolves."

Discernment & Decision Making

Colossians 2:8 "Beware lest any man spoil you through philosophy and vain deceit, after the tradition of men, after the rudiments of the world, and not after Christ."

1 John 4:1 "Beloved, believe not every spirit, but try the spirits whether they are of God: because many false prophets are gone out into the world."

Satan was very convincing, believable, and seemingly helpful to Eve's situation. He knew what God said, and he knew what Eve wanted, so he encouraged her to serve herself the lust of her heart on a silver platter. I wonder how long she just stared at the forbidden tree before Satan came along with his brand of *caring* advice?

She relied upon her own reasoning, coupled with satanic advice, and forsook the Word of God in the process.

Then she gave to her husband, and he listened to his wife instead of following the Word of God. He was to lead, but instead he followed his wife into an ungodly and unwise decision that was very costly, not only for them, but for the entire human race to follow.

They broke the first principle of discernment and decision making. That principle is: **once God has given a command on any subject, there is no decision to be made**. The only thing to do is what God has already said to do, or not to do. There is no room for reasoning.

Adam took all of the knowledge that he had from God, listened to his wife, who listened to Satan, the outside source, and took his subtle and twisted counsel. From there they embarked on a sin-tainted journey, which is still affecting all of mankind in a terrible way.

Discernment & Decision Making

If your child asks for addictive drugs, what would you say? You would say no! Why? Because you know they would be harmful to them. You know the probability of addiction and the dangerous short-term and long-term effects of drug use. You know the further problems that can happen while under the influence of drugs. You know addictive drugs are not good for anyone. It is an easy conclusion to make. It is an easy command for you to give to your child. You know what is best for them.

When you ask for something that is bad for you, God will say no. That is because He knows best. He is **the** KNOW IT ALL! He can see across time. He realizes the harm that will come from you getting what you want. So He says "No." Man may not understand the rules and regulations of God. Yet to know God is to learn that He indeed is a caring Father that knows best.

Proverbs 6:27 "Can a man take fire in his bosom, and his clothes not be burned?"

[Genesis 3:6—10] Once they got what they wanted, they felt the conviction and shame as a result of their bad decision. They hid themselves from God, which shows that they knew they had done wrong. This was a lustful, selfish, self-serving decision that was made without vision. The long term effects and / or consequence were outrageous and inconceivable. Yet we find they were self-inflicted wounds. They made an unnecessary decision.

> We should never stress about making a **made** decision.

Most of the time when people are making a decision, the determining factor is their present want. They have failed to calculate and consider how their decision may affect them and others with them, over time.

Discernment & Decision Making

Adam and Eve were kicked out of the Garden of Eden. It was the garden of real paradise and ease. There was no going back once they realized they made a bad decision. They became impoverished, or spiritually bankrupt, destitute, and deficient. They lost everything they had and all they had ever known. They had to work among the thorns of life for every morsel of bread they would eat. Why? Because they made the worst decision they could have made.

They had NO VISION. They were affected; their children were affected, and every man, woman, boy, and girl who have ever lived have been affected by the decision of Adam and Eve to eat the forbidden fruit. They certainly did not consider you and me, any more than they considered their own children. Most importantly they did not consider God.

> Proverbs 29:18 "Where *there is* no **vision**, the people perish: but he that keepeth **the law**, happy *is* he."

Notice that a lack of vision is directly attached to or associated with keeping the law. When we set aside the Word of God, we set aside our vision. We hide the very light which is given to illuminate and brighten the path we are to travel in this life.

> Psalm 119:105 NUN. "Thy word *is* a lamp unto my feet, and a light unto my path."

Without vision, people perish. The outcome or aftermath of Adam and Eve's decision exhibits or illustrates the great tragedy of what happens when there is a lack of vision. We must have vision in our decision making. That means we must be Biblical in our decision making. We must first consider how a decision will affect our relationship with God. Then we must consider others, and lastly, ourselves. The blessings of the long term will be more beneficial when we make Biblical decisions than the short term gratification we often seek at the expense of true blessings. Adam and Eve were very short-sighted in the decision they made.

Look at the fallout of their very selfish decision which should have never been considered, much less made. [Genesis 3:8—24] God knew the short term and long term effects of eating the forbidden fruit. That is why He issued His warning to them. They were restricted from the Garden of Eden forever. There would be hard work and labor for all mankind. The effects of sin for most will be eternally felt.

[Genesis 3:16, 17] Sin fell upon all men, and from that time forward, God gave man to rule over the woman. Her bad decision was to eat what God said not to eat. Adam's bad decision was to follow his wife by eating what God said not to eat. He was not deceived; he knew better than to do what he did.

2Corinthians 11:3 "But I fear, lest by any means, as the serpent beguiled Eve through his subtilty, so your minds should be corrupted from the simplicity that is in Christ." [1 Timothy 2:9—15]

The transaction of bad behavior on their parts contributed to how the family and the church are to be ruled. When there is a decision to violate God's order and structure for the home, there will be problems.

**Do you have a decision to make
...or has it been made for you?**

CHAPTER FOUR
Stop signs are there for a reason

Cain and Abel: Genesis 4:1—15

When we come upon a stop sign, we must realize that it is there for a reason. It is communicating a very important message to us. A message we **must** heed. The stop sign does not respect one person over another. It is an equalizer to all those who travel that way. The message of the stop sign is not optional. It is letting the driver know that there is cross traffic, which may, or may not have a stop sign of their own, at that particular intersection. Whether they do or not, it is no matter to them, for they have no option, since a stop sign is facing them, they must stop. They have been warned. If they stop they will protect their life, the life of those traveling with them and the lives of those traveling in the other direction.

The first thing we can see in the story of Cain and Abel is that Cain had an incomplete relationship with God. Pharaoh had the same problem [Exodus 5:1, 2]. Because he did not know God, he did not seem to fully know, or understand, what God wanted or expected of him. Or, he just did not care. [Genesis 4:6, 7] God tried to warn him about the cross traffic, but he failed to listen to the counsel of God. Most likely it was a result of his relationship with God not being what it should have been.

Cain was the older brother. He should have been a good leader by setting the example for his younger brother. Instead his younger brother was setting the example for him to follow. That must have stirred and fueled his emotions; that coupled with God's denial and rebuke of his unacceptable sacrifice provoked him to sin further, or continue in his sin.

Proverbs 13:1 "A wise son *heareth* his father's instruction: but a scorner heareth not rebuke."

Proverbs 10:8 "The wise in heart will receive commandments: but a prating fool shall fall."

Proverbs 12:15 "The way of a fool *is* right in his own eyes: but he that hearkeneth unto counsel *is* wise."

Proverbs 13:16 "Every prudent *man* dealeth with knowledge: but a fool layeth open *his* folly."

Proverbs 17:10 "A reproof entereth more into a wise man than an hundred stripes into a fool."

Proverbs 17:16 "Wherefore *is there* a price in the hand of a fool to get wisdom, seeing *he hath* no heart *to it?*"

Cain's failure to listen to God, after his first mistake, which was an unacceptable sacrifice, lead to his second bad decision, which was the killing of his brother. One bad decision led to another. He showed himself a fool by rejecting God's gracious counsel. He became an example to all of us.

Hebrews 11:4 "By faith Abel offered unto God a more excellent sacrifice than Cain, by which he obtained witness that he was righteous, God testifying of his gifts: and by it he being dead yet speaketh." [1John 3:12; Jude 1:11]

Cain complicated and compounded the problem by refusing to accept his own failure. He could have made the right change in his worship and moved forward in building a right relationship with God. He is like most people who will often try to cover up their wrong, because they do not want to be exposed or seen as wrong or a failure. They try to dispose of their wrong in some way. Their second wrong will never make the first wrong go away [2 Samuel 11 and 12]. David found this to be true.

Cain became emotional, and thereby allowed bitterness and envy to become his enemies. These would then work internally to bring irreparable destruction to his life. His emotions got the best of him. This made him an easy target and caused him to make a hasty and very bad decision. In anger and swiftness he killed his own brother.

John 8:44 "Ye are of your father the devil, and the lusts of your father ye will do. He was a murderer from the beginning, and abode not in the truth, because there is no truth in him. When he speaketh a lie, he speaketh of his own: for he is a liar, and the father of it."

[Some people work to destroy others with evil words. They will do a character assassination of someone. Most likely this is done in an effort to make them look better by comparison.]

Cain's first decision was about what he did without proper regard to what God wanted or expected from him. His second bad decision was very selfish and pointless. His brother had nothing to do with his first decision, and his brother did nothing to provoke his second decision. He could not see things clearly because he only saw or considered himself. He ended up compromising himself in the long term to get what he wanted in the short term.

He would have been wise to humble himself and accept failure for the bad and wrong sacrifice, which he alone made. If he had humbled himself at God's rebuke, there would not have been a second bad decision. He would not have killed his brother in an effort to satisfy his own failure. His brother did him no wrong; Cain wronged himself.

It is amazing how many people will bring other people into their problem. Cain could not allow his brother Abel to look better than him. When Cain failed himself he chose to live by *the devilish philosophy* of working to eliminate the competition. [Daniel 6] Daniel faced the same type of wicked thinkers and evil doers. The Pharisees worked the same devilish plan when it came to Jesus, whom they saw as a threat to themselves. If Cain thought that killing his brother would make him feel better, he was wrong. *Instant gratification* does not usually bring long-term peace. Our peace comes because of foundational things in our spirit and not by temporal things executed in or by our flesh.

Another issue to consider is the fact that Cain did not take personal responsibility for his conduct in bad decision number one. Then he did not take personal responsibility for bad decision number two: 'Am I my brother's keeper?" He obviously realized he was wrong because instead of facing the issue, he ran. Most people who have done no wrong do not need to hide. They stand and face the issue. That would be the act or response of an honorable man.

When we do wrong, we must own up to that wrong by facing the consequence, seeking forgiveness and grace from God and from those whom we have offended. For instance, if two people have a child out of wedlock, they will do better in the long term to face the consequence of their bad decision so that the bad decision is not made worse.

The long term effects on Cain and his family were more than he could bear. The consequence should have been more closely considered **before** he did what he did. He should have considered the cost **before**, and then he would have realized his decision would cost more than he had to pay. Cain had terrible discernment. He did not know God, and therefore he made a very bad decision, times two.

The price is always going to be higher than we can afford.

The thing that I would say in closing about Cain is that he became who he was over a period of time and not all at once. He had rebellious tendencies all along the way. He was not prone to listen to authority, and therefore he was predisposed to make multiple bad decisions. We can learn good things from Cain's bad decisions.

In the short term, stopping at a stop sign might seem like an inconvenience to your fast-paced life. It can seem like a bother to your agenda. It can be considered as an impediment to where you want to go. However, in the long term stopping is the best idea when you consider the consequence for not stopping for the high speed traffic traveling the other direction. An accident is certainly an inconvenience and an impediment you cannot change or afford.

CHAPTER FIVE
Did Noah have a choice?

Noah and the Ark Genesis 6:8, 11—13

Do you believe Noah had a choice as to whether or not he was going to follow God and build an ark? Does Scripture present Noah's building of the ark as a choice? How did Noah hear the instructions God gave him?

The Word of God teaches that Noah had no choice. Scripture does not teach that Noah thought or acted like he had a choice. Noah took God's instruction as a command. There was no option for his family. If he was to save his family he had to follow God no matter what He asked. Father knows best. That issue must be settled in our hearts as it was in Noah's. It was a principle by which Noah lived.

God laid an overwhelming task upon Noah. This task would take 100 years to accomplish. It took a commitment from Noah. He would lead his family to follow the will of God. {I have wondered if Noah had to plant trees and wait for them to grow so he could harvest them, before he could finish the ark.}

The instructions that God gives us to have a healthy marriage and raise a godly family will take years. It is a daily commitment. It is a labor of love. It will take eighteen, twenty years, or maybe more, to raise children and till death to enjoy marriage. It is a process that will take a commitment, patience, time and following God's instructions in obedience.

[Genesis 6:14] God's instruction to Noah was not stated as the eleventh commandment; **but** it was not

Discernment & Decision Making

stated as an option or opinion from God either. I would ask you to observe verse 17, 18, where God gives Noah the alternative. It was not offered as a choice, but as a warning. At first it almost appears as a request. It is presented as a good idea with a reward. Notice that God uses the phrase: "thou **shalt** come."

It was a command. God gave Noah and his family favor and showed them mercy. He presented everything to them in the best possible light, as being a great idea, as one they should take, and the conclusion is, this was a command. [Genesis 7:5, 9, 16]

There is no decision presented by God. God made up Noah's mind for him and decided the thing that was best for Noah and his family. Taking the ark God offered brought them safety and preservation. God was not giving Noah a suggestion, or offering Noah His opinion as **a best-guess-take-it-or-leave-it option; this was a command right from the beginning**!

I stress this point because the truth is that many of our decisions are made for us by GOD. There is no choice to be considered, pondered, or reasoned where God has made our choice for us. To those who were saved, **going into the flood was no choice.** In most cases God has already made our choice for us. **When you treat non-decisions as decisions you will most likely find yourself in a flood of trouble.**

Like me, my children are confronted with decisions each day. As their parent, I will make most of their decisions for them. In such cases they have no decision to make. Many of the decisions that I will make for them are decisions God has made for them. I am instructing them that God has made certain decisions for all of us.

Other decisions they will not make until they are released from my immediate care and responsibility. That is not at age thirteen, but as long as they are in my home, I will make many decisions for them. While they live with me I will teach them how to make their own decisions. Little by little I will let them make decisions. When they make a bad decision I am there to help them deal with it.

The truth is that God has made many decisions for all of us. Yet many Christians will treat almost all of the statutes, judgments, and instruction of God, given to us in HIS WORD, as optional. How could you ever think that you could improve upon anything that God has stated, whether as a direct command, a principle, a pattern or model for the best way to live?

Let me give an incomplete list of things where God has made our decisions for us:

There is no decision regarding church attendance. God made your decision for you.

Hebrews 10:25 "Not forsaking the assembling of ourselves together, as the manner of some *is*; but exhorting *one another*: and so much the more, as ye see the day approaching."

There is no decision regarding your tithe. God made your decision for you.

Malachi 3:10 "Bring ye all the tithes into the storehouse, that there may be meat in mine house, and prove me now herewith, saith the LORD of hosts, if I will not open you the windows of heaven, and pour you out a blessing, that *there shall* not *be room* enough *to receive it*."

Discernment & Decision Making

1 Corinthians 16:2 "Upon the first *day* of the week let every one of you lay by him in store, as *God* hath prospered him, that there be no gatherings when I come."

It is the same with leadership in the home.
God made your decision for you.

Ephesians 5:25 "Husbands, love your wives, even as Christ also loved the church, and gave himself for it;"

Colossians 3:19 "Husbands, love *your* wives, and be not bitter against them."

Ephesians 5:22 "Wives, submit yourselves unto your own husbands, as unto the Lord."

Colossians 3:18 "Wives, submit yourselves unto your own husbands, as it is fit in the Lord."

Ephesians 6:1 "Children, obey your parents in the Lord: for this is right."

Colossians 3:20 "Children, obey *your* parents in all things: for this is well pleasing unto the Lord."

How to discipline your children-
God made your decision for you.

Proverbs 19: 18 "Chasten thy son while there is hope, and let not thy soul spare for his crying." [Proverbs 13:24; 23:13; 29:17]

Regarding salvation God made your decision for you.

Acts 17:30 "And the times of this ignorance God winked at; but now **commandeth** all men every where to repent:"

Romans 10:16 "But they have not all obeyed the gospel. For Esaias saith, Lord, who hath believed our report?"

A command is not an option; it is a command.

It is the same with many other sins like lying, adultery, bitterness, drinking, envy, sorcery, homosexuality, stealing, laziness, and divorce. Any time God gives His word on a subject, we must follow His instruction to the letter.

We are instructed to be content with what we have, and we are told not to covet. We are instructed when and how to use anger. We are told that we should treat others like we want to be treated, and we are told that if we do not work, we should not eat.

There are so many things that we do not have to decide because God has given instruction directly, or in some cases, indirectly. This is true with subjects like smoking and gambling or whether you should send your children to a public school. God established the issue of learning, but God **did not** establish the Godless public school system as our avenue for learning. I believe you can find the principles in the Bible that can answer any decision you need to make. Knowing God's Word is very important to making all decisions.

If you do not follow God's instructions regarding any issue that God has already decided, then you can expect a flood of trouble that you will likely be unable to bear. You will not arrive safely on shore; you most likely will perish in the flood, **if you have rejected a decision God made for you**. Father does know best.

Too many people look at the instructions of the Bible as advice that they can follow or reject. They have been given no such liberty from God. All the statues, judgments, standards, and instructions from the Word of God are meant to be followed completely. Could a person possibly think they are smarter than God?

You might not receive the penalty in this life for breaking the laws of old, such as being stoned for adultery or rebellion to parents, but adultery and rebellion are still just as wrong as they ever were. These sins will never be in style with God. Your salvation is not determined by keeping the law, but everything in the law is still good government to live by. Jesus came to fulfill the law. He accomplished what no one else could do, and the laws of old will still provide for right living.

It is high time that God's people quit looking at the instructions of God's Word as optional. They should stop treating the Word of God like a smorgasbord, picking and choosing what they like and disregarding the rest. That is pure nonsense and foolish thinking.

Is it any wonder the world does not fear GOD as they should when the people of GOD do not seem to fear the GOD whom they say they love! It is no wonder the world looks at the Word of God and the things of God as optional instead of **The Book** to be obeyed.

John 14:15 "If ye love me, keep my commandments."

44

Discernment & Decision Making

Noah feared and openly obeyed God. He uncompromisingly preached the truth of God for 100 years. He received no accolades, applause, or praise from man. He continued to do right no matter whether anyone else in the entire world listened and obeyed God. That should be our testimony in this wicked world. We should listen and obey God as though we have no choice whatsoever. The truth is, when it comes right down to it, **God knows best. We cannot improve on what God knows.** We have no good choice but to obey God.

Noah did not believe he had a choice. So he complied completely and whole heartedly with God's command, from the first board he cut, until he lead his entire family into that ark of God's safety. As far as he was concerned, this was not up for reasoning, discussion, or debate. The building of the ark was given and received as a command.

Did Noah have a choice? No! Noah had no choice. His decision was made for him, by God, and it was the best decision when compared with dying in a flood. It was the best decision for his family and himself. It secured the continuation of civilization in this world. It saved life.

It was a decision of faith. He believed in a rain storm he had never seen. He believed it would last for forty days and forty nights and cover the earth. Noah believed in a world-wide flood, and because he believed, he acted upon his belief in the Word of GOD!

We must believe in God and let Him make all of our decisions for us. Whether the decisions we are confronted with are clearly spelled out in the Word of God, or whether it is a principle defined in the Word of God, or it is a decision about buying or selling, staying or going. We must consider God in prayer for each and every one. **God does know best and we cannot improve on what God knows**. What we will find is a rainbow of safety and security in the promises of God. You can take that to the ark.

CHAPTER SIX
Faithful decisions

Genesis 12:1—9

Abraham lived by faith. In many respects he could be considered the father of faith. He made the BIGGEST decisions he would ever make, for himself and his household, based solely upon his faith in God. By faith he allowed God to charter his course **from what he knew** to the unknown plains of the future. He went into a horizon he could not yet see beyond all because God said He would make a great nation out of him. He obeyed God by faith.

Abraham made this life changing decision at age SEVENTY-FIVE. He left everything he knew about. He left most of his family and friends. He left familiar surroundings and set out to go to a place which he had never seen. He uprooted his household to accept THE promise of God. It was a decision he made by faith.

This decision he made would surely seem certifiably insane to most people, especially at that time in history. At that time family and familiar surroundings were everything. Travelling long distance was very difficult. There was no chartering a plane to enjoy a time of furlough. His decision would be classified as crazy by the lost and by many of those who call themselves Christians.

This was a major decision that altered his entire existence. It was made as a result of his **faith** in God. His faith in God was Abraham's guiding force, and IT changed his life and the lives of many others, forever.

The Christian life is a life based entirely upon faith. It is a life that is meant to be lived out in faith. The world

47

does not understand, nor can they comprehend the way we live, or at least the way we should live, our lives. A man leaving his homeland because God told him to is a matter of faith which will not make earthly, temporal sense to the lost.

[Hebrews 11:3, 6, 28, 33, 39] Through faith in God, is the manner which the Old Testament saints lived their lives. They made life changing decisions that set the course for their life, both now and for their eternity. They lived "through faith" in the God of heaven. In so doing they pleased God. This is the very purpose for which all men were created [Revelation 4:11]. **If** we are to please God above all else, we must live totally by faith.

> Acts 3:16 "And his name through faith in his name hath made this man strong, whom ye see and know: yea, the faith which is by him hath given him this **perfect soundness** in the presence of you all."

We find this man was healed and his life was altered and changed for the better through faith in Christ. He went from a life of hopelessness, which was filled with doubt and confusion, and he was given a life of perfect or complete soundness of mind, through faith in Jesus Christ.

> Romans 3:25 "Whom God hath set forth *to be* a propitiation through faith in his blood, to declare his righteousness for the remission of sins that are past, through the forbearance of God;"

We are saved **through faith** in the *physically* unseen God.

2 Timothy 3:15 "And that from a child thou hast known the holy scriptures, which are able to make thee wise unto salvation through faith which is in Christ Jesus."

Ephesians 2:8 "For by grace are ye saved through faith; and that not of yourselves: *it is* the gift of God:"

[2 Peter 1:3—5] We went from hopelessness to become partakers of the divine nature. It is a wonderfully eternal turn of events and all of it through, by, and because of faith. Faith is meant to be our guide. [Galatians 3:8, 14] Through faith we receive `all` the promises of GOD.

1 Peter 1:5 "Who are **kept** by the power of God through faith unto salvation ready to be revealed in the last time." We are kept, through faith. That means that faith does not only work for salvation and for our eternity but we are also kept here and now by faith.

If we are saved, we made that life-changing decision by faith. We have made eternal decisions by, through, and in faith. We have put our faith and trust in the God of the universe whom we have never seen. So then, how is it that the everyday decisions we make should be made by sight?

The God of the Bible and the God of eternity does not want to be relegated to the God of salvation. He does not desire to be kept in your spiritual closet, attic, or garage until you need Him. He wants to be and should be our GOD everyday!

Discernment & Decision Making

Because of position and experience, God has earned the right to be *the decision maker* for every aspect of our lives. In addition, we are bought with a price, and we are no longer our own. He is the Master, and we are the certified servant saint. He is the Saviour, and we are the saved. We must yield to Him in everything.

We understand that God has a grand plan that He is working in eternity. His people are the tools and vessels that He uses to accomplish His work, here on earth. Using sanctified people is the way God designed His work to be accomplished. [2 Timothy 2:21]

That is why we must be available and ready to be utilized by Him. We must be on call, for His purpose, in His time, so that His work can be completed through us. When we go our own way and do our own thing, we are not just hurting our life or the life of our family, but we are affecting or causing delay to the work of God. We must ask God what to do about everything so He can direct and manage all the details of our lives. How do you ask God to help you get back when you get to where you moved if you did not ask and get an answer as to whether you should have gone in the first place; very humbly. Every decision we make should be in accordance with the will of God.

We must ask God how we should spend our time, and we must be available to His call wherever we go. Remember that God is always looking to the long term, whereas most people look to what will affect them here and now. If we ask God, He can and will help keep us stay in tune with *eternal thinking,* and hence, all of our decisions will be made with eternity in focus. We will have our affection stayed on eternity as we look to God with

50

every decision. We will become *eternally-minded* as we ask God to make all of our decisions for us.

[Genesis 12:10—20] The famine came, and Abraham left where God brought him. The only time Abraham brought trouble upon himself and into his home was when he made this decision seemingly by sight. He left the promise-land by sight, and when he did, he began to make decisions by fear, seemingly setting aside his life-changing faith.

Abraham looks to have made a *panic decision* because of what he saw. While he was there he seems to have forgotten the promises of God upon his life. As a result, he made more bad decisions when he arrived in Egypt, far away from the promise-land and the will of God. By hiding the whole truth, he showed doubt in the promises of God. How many times do we act in this same way?

> There was no way he could die as long
> as God's promise to him was unfulfilled

We must be very careful when making decisions during *famine-type troubles*. These are usually the times when we are most likely to get off the beaten path of faith, by making fearful plans by sight. Many of our bad decisions are made in faithless self-preservation. Abraham lied to save his life, which needed no salvation. God was the one to protect Abraham and His promises to him.

Was it kindhearted and loving to take his wife through Egypt as his sister? Was that the most loving, considerate, and kind thing to do? When we take our loved ones through bad decisions, is it kind-hearted, loving, and considerate? Are we treating our loved ones properly or selfishly when we take them through bad decisions?

Did Adam do the very best for his wife and himself when he ate the forbidden? Did Lot do the best for his wife and family when he moved to Sodom? Did Achan do the very best for his wife and family with his decision to take the accursed? Did Ananias do the best for Sapphira to lie to the Holy Spirit? What kinds of things are you putting your loved ones through because of your bad, *anti-faith* decisions?

Once again I state; **if** God is good enough to chart the course of our eternity, **if** He can be trusted with the greatest of all decisions we will ever make, then He must be well able to guide our everyday decisions. If God can plan for us in eternity past, and He can see our eternity future, then He certainly can be trusted with the day-to-day operations of your life and mine.

[Genesis 13:1—4] Sight got Abraham off course, and faith got Abraham back on track. He might have learned a lesson in Egypt, but he lost time. We too will bring setbacks into our life as we get off course and travel by sight. We have a Bible, backed by a loving God to help us chart our course of faith. We can rely on God's strength. We have a heavenly Father to give us guidance and direction. We shall never fail as we obey God. Those who are lost have no such hope or help.

Our God is a God of order and structure. By and through faith in God, we should make our decisions and build a structured life that will ever be in harmony with the Father. We will find the abundant promises of God to be true and faithful. He makes it possible for us to live at peace. Let God decide your course.

CHAPTER SEVEN
Avoid hasty and emotional decisions

The story of Abraham, Sarai, and Hagar

Genesis 16:1—6

This story exhibits and highlights classic mistakes in bad decision making. Many times we can see a pattern, when people make a wrong decision. This story also shows the classic *domino effect* when a bad decision is made. Our bad decisions will affect our life and the lives of others.

I feel compelled to remind you that these stories are here for us to learn from so we do not make the same exact, or the same kind of mistakes the people in the Bible made. These stories are good for us because we can see what happens over time when a bad decision is made. We are privileged to see thousands of year's worth of trouble from some of the most costly decisions, possibly ever made, and then truthfully and accurately recorded for the entire world to see and read. We must learn from their mistakes in decision making.

The Bible is filled with true, real-life stories. These are real people, and their names have not been hidden. The story is not fictitious, nor is it embellished for theatrical or dramatic affect. We should take notes as we study Bible stories.

Romans 15:4 "For whatsoever things were written aforetime were written **for our learning**, that we through patience and comfort of the scriptures might have hope." [1 Corinthians 10:1—11; 2 Timothy 3:16-17]

Discernment & Decision Making

God is gracious to us. He has given us careful instructions, detailed throughout His Word, on how to live life. He has also told us, or warned us, to pay very close attention to the decisions and mistakes that our Biblical forefathers have made. God has told us to learn from them, so we can avoid the pitfalls that impacted, detoured, and in some cases, swallowed up their lives. That is why this story of Abraham and Sarah is here. The only way this story goes to waste in your life or mine is when we fail to heed its warning.

The first thing we can see in this story is the lack of trust in God's Word. They could not see how God would fulfill His promises. They concluded they were too old for God to use in the manner God had chosen. They must have doubted God would do what He said He would do in the way He said He would. They could not see the God of the impossible.

Because they doubted God, they designed an alternative plan. In their eyes, it was a 'better' or quicker way of getting a descendant. In the process they would **help** God keep His promise to them. They designed a way that they thought would work, and they would make God's promise fit into their design. There would be an heir one way or the other.

As Christians, whenever we fail to conduct our marriages and raise our children in a Biblical way, we show our distrust for God's Word. Many people treat the Bible as old fashion, archaic, or they misapply it to their life. We show that we doubt the promises of God, whole-heartily, when we dismiss God's word, as if we feel it does not apply to our life. If we do, we will experience hurt in our lives and lead our family into failure.

Abram and Sarai did not whole-heartily trust God, and as a result, they did not rely upon God alone to handle the situation. They wanted the promise NOW, and therefore they did not WAIT upon God. They put their dependence in an alternative solution. They failed to abide by rule number one. Rule number one is always rule number one, and it never cease to be rule number one, no matter what we might see. Are you ready to hear rule number one?

1 Samuel 15:22 "And Samuel said, Hath the LORD [as great] delight in burnt offerings and sacrifices, as in obeying the voice of the LORD? Behold, **to obey** *is* **better than sacrifice**, *and* to hearken than the fat of rams."

[Proverbs 21:3; Ecclesiastes 5:1; Isaiah 1:11-17; Jeremiah 7:22-23; Hosea 6:6; Micah 6:6-8; Matthew 5:24; 9:13]

Keeping God's word is our first and foremost duty. Increase is never our duty. Making the will of God come to pass in our life, or the life of another, is not our duty. Sowing seed is our duty, and if it is ever to happen for us, then God will determine the place and time. Therefore all decisions should be made by God, for God, with God, and then God will determine how, when, and where. His time and place will always be accurate.

The story of Mary & Joseph illustrates this truth.

Micah 5:2 "But thou, Bethlehem Ephratah, *though* thou be little among the thousands of Judah, *yet* out of thee shall he come forth unto me *that is* to be ruler in Israel; whose goings forth *have been* from of old, from everlasting."

Matthew 2:1 "Now when Jesus was born in Bethlehem of Judaea in the days of Herod the king, behold, there came wise men from the east to Jerusalem,"

Joseph and Mary were forced to go to Bethlehem so that the baby Jesus could be born at **the time and place God said He would be born.** This was a fulfillment of God's Word.

Next, we see that Abram received bad counsel from his wife. By taking her counsel, Abram made a very bad decision that affected both of them, as well as all of their descendants to come. It would seem that this became an emotional decision instead of a well thought out godly decision based solely in the Word of God.

Sarai's emotions were high as she tried to *wait* upon God, without seeing the physical growth of a child. She was asked to believe God and over a period of time, her desire to have a baby, which she could hold in her arms, became emotionally overwhelming. She went to Abram and poured out her heart, and Abram must have been moved by the passion of his wife. Her emotions became more powerful and more important than the promise of God. They acted by sight in that moment without having proper vision.

[Genesis 15:1—6] Abram went against his own belief. He came to the point where he believed God, but when it came to the feelings of his wife, he set aside the Word of God, overcome by her sentiment. Emotions change, but the Word of God does not move from its place. The foundation of our life is to be the Holy Scriptures. We are not to be moved by the winds of changing doctrines or the fads of our time, or the emotions we feel. We must not go against the Word of GOD, no matter what!

Psalm 119: 105 "Thy word is **a lamp** unto my feet, and **a light** unto my path." [Proverbs 6:23]

Many Christians make life-changing decisions based upon the barometer of their feelings. When people's emotions are tied up or entangled in any situation, many times people will set aside the Word of God because they are not thinking clearly, but are guided by their emotions.

We must not look to the circumstance,
but we must seek to do what the BIBLE says.

James 1:13 "Let no man say when he is tempted, I am tempted of God: for God cannot be tempted with evil, neither tempteth he any man: 14 But every man is tempted, when he is drawn away of his own lust, and enticed. 15 Then when lust hath conceived, it bringeth forth sin: and sin, when it is finished, bringeth forth death."

We often hear these verses used in associated with sexual sins. That is because when we think of **lust**, we relate it with sexuality, and it is, or can be. However, when Sarai **lusted** for a baby, she was led away or drawn away by her lust. What was she drawn away from? It was the Word of God.

LUST, n. 1. Longing desire; eagerness to possess or enjoy; as the lust of gain. My lust shall be satisfied upon them. Ex. 15. 2. Concupiscence; carnal appetite; unlawful desire of carnal pleasure. Romans 1. 2 Peter 2. 3. Evil propensity; depraved affections and desires. James 1. Ps. 81. 4. Vigor; active power. [Not used.]

Noah Webster's 1828 Dictionary

LUST involves other things besides just sexual matters.

It is important for us to understand and accept that the baby they were to have would be for God. This baby was not for self gratification, but this was about fulfilling the will of God. This was not Sarai's or Abram's matter to control; this was God's working. This baby was to fulfill the plan of GOD, and these parents were mere vessels used to fulfill the will of God!

Psalm 127:3 "Lo, children *are* an heritage of the LORD: *and* the fruit of the womb *is His* reward." The children belong to GOD; check with Him. Worry about your own children."

Sarai was emotionally charged; then she charged up Abram's emotions. They both sinned, as they were led, or drawn away, from the Word of God, and the promise of God, by working to fulfill their own lust.

Most of the time there is an inability to undo bad decisions. Once a bad decision is made the consequence of that bad decision will eventually be realized. We have heard this truth many times, but do we understand the passage:

Galatians 6:7 "Be not deceived; God is not mocked: for whatsoever a man soweth, that shall he also reap." Do you take that promise seriously?

The conflict that results from this decision is yet ongoing in Israel today thousands of years later. There were, and still are, long-term effects that are with the Jewish people to this day. The Ishmaelites still claim Abraham as their father, too. They still fight for the inheritance that Abraham passed to Isaac and Jacob. Ishmael was sent away as a mocker.

> Israel belongs to God, but try and tell that to the Ishmaelites today and see if they will listen.

This decision was very, very costly. The price is still being paid, and it will continue to be paid until Jesus comes. He will be the One to fix the dispute over the land, and to settle the matter of the inheritance that was promised to Isaac, Jacob or Israel, and to their children.

[Genesis 16:7—9] I also would have you notice that Sarai talked her husband into this bad decision. Then she takes it out on Hagar, her maidservant. Then Hagar makes a bad decision and runs away. The moral of this story is that our bad decisions will affect the lives of others.

[Genesis 16:15, 16; 17:1] It also disrupted Abram's fellowship with God. One day he was talking with God, and He takes Abram outside and tells him the story of the stars, explaining His promise to him, and then one day God stops talking to him. Silence was not golden, but a hazy dark.

It would be almost fourteen years, as far as we know, before God would speak to Abram after he made a decision not to trust in God. He is God of the universe, Creator of everything, and He hand-picked a man to make a promise, only to have that man receive counsel from his wife, who was able to talk Abram out of the promise God made to him, as though He had not made the promise or was unable to fulfill the promise He made. Sad was the story. How many times has that been true in our lives?

Abram had in fact told God, by his actions, that he did not believe God. You might think God is not affected by your decisions to go against His Word, but I believe you would be wrong. He does care. Fourteen years go by before God talks to Abram again.

CHAPTER EIGHT
"It was well watered every where..."

Lot and Abraham: [Genesis 13:5—12]

"And Lot lifted up his eyes, and beheld all the plain of Jordan, that it was well watered every where..."

Lot saw what he wanted to see as he examined the plains of Jordan. He probably had to overlook some things to see the "well watered" plains. He had been with uncle Abram, and he might have grown tired of the dusty plains. As far as he was concerned, it was time for a change of pace. It is also relative to mention that something led to Lot moving away.

There had obviously been a struggle of discontentment and restlessness between the camp of Abram and Lot's men. It came time to separate one from the other in order to save the peace. Up until now, Lot had followed Abram out of Ur and across the plains. This division opened up his first opportunity to set out on his own to do his own thing. Like the average come-of-age-teenager, he was finally able to choose his course of "freedom." [Luke 15:11-19]

[Genesis 13:13] I wonder if Lot knew anything about Sodom before he made this life-changing decision for his family. Had Lot heard rumors about the kinds of things going on in Sodom? Had he heard about or seen the types of people who resided there? Did he know anything about Sodom, and is that why he went there?

Because even if he did not know, he should have tried to find out something about that place before he moved in that direction? Maybe he should have taken a survey trip to find out what Sodom was like. He could have talked to the people of Sodom. He seemingly went without knowing or discovering the real dangers for his family, until it was too late? That is never a good idea.

This might have been his first major decision. He had been under the care and concern of his uncle, but now he would branch out on his own. It was his first taste of independence. So how did his first decision turn out? [Genesis 19:1—14] He moved to a place that God had plans to destroy. Not really a smart idea.

[Genesis 18:20] Lot traded his tent for a townhouse, so to speak. His decision making took him past the plain and into the city of Sodom. It was so very wicked and sinful, that along with Gomorrah, God decided to annihilate Sodom as though it never was.

[Genesis 19:7, 8] His thinking and his decision making were so messed up that Lot thought to give his *virgin* daughters to the men of that city, Sodom, to pacify their deviant, vile, and insatiable appetite of sinful lust. [2Peter 2:7-8] Their conversation, or manner of life, ruined Lot's thinking in the 20-plus years he lived there.

[Genesis 19:14] Lot was so tainted by sin that he even lost credibility with his sons-in-law. [Genesis 19:16] Even after Lot knew the city was to be destroyed, he still *lollie-gagged* and lingered in that very sinful place. He and his family had obviously become very fond of *Sodom life.*

[Genesis 19: 17—20, 30—37] We find here more devastating and disastrous decisions. Lot may have started as a just man, but he became unjust along the way, and we see the results of his bad decisions.

It is obvious to us, now knowing what we know, that Lot made a very, very bad decision, which lead to additional bad decisions. We see this because we are in the position of having 20/20 hindsight. We have viewed the ruins and the aftermath of his horrible decision, and we can see his failures, as we pick through the destruction of his life. Lot was focused on the wrong things.

Matthew 6:33 "But seek ye **first** the kingdom of God, and **his** righteousness; and all these things shall be added unto you."

His righteousness **must** be our **MAIN** focus and pursuit. **ALL** of our decisions must come from that pursuit. If it is not in accordance with righteousness, then what is it that we seek to achieve?

We can **now** see that Lot lost children to the devouring fires of life in Sodom. We can see that he lost his wife when she turned back for one more *'precious'* look at the city that she had grown to love so very much, so much so that she was willing to commit suicide for it, even after that city took her family from her. Then we see that Lot's daughters got him drunk and had their way with their father, because of their perverted and twisted thinking. Is it any wonder they thought as they did, after their father offered them to the perverts of Sodom. Lot became father to his own grandsons.

We have the present-day advantage of Bible knowledge, with 20/20 Biblical hindsight, to see and know that Lot's decisions turned out very bad for Lot and his family. He acquired consequences that were more than he could have expected when he first saw and lusted for the: "well watered" plain of Jordan.

"And Lot lifted up his eyes, and **beheld** all the plain of Jordan, that it was well watered every where..." Genesis 13:10 [1 John 2:15—17]

At the time Lot made his decision, it might have seemed like a great idea. He might have thought it would bring great economic stability and progressive opportunities for his family. His wife and children might be able to have more and do a little 'better'. They could sell their raggedy-old tent and buy a home in the city. They could buy or lease a brand new camel. Things were looking up for Lot and his family.

What **if** this situation were in modern-day times with current lingo? What would it look and sound like? If Lot took the new job in Sodom, he could provide 'better' things for his family. His wife and children could make some new friends. He could enroll his children in bigger and better schools, like Sodom High, with its great academically accredited program, state-of-the-art sports program, with cheerleading and dance classes available. There are great restaurants, financial increase, nice malls, outlet stores and a Starbucks on every corner throughout the city.

There was no talk of a good church. "Lot, what about God! Where will your children go to church, Lot? Where will they hear the Word of God?" Abraham most likely had been Lot's connection to God; but now where and how will God's message come to them? What church would they go to in Sodom?

What if you were given the opportunity to move?

The decision Lot made seems to have been based on looks. It was a physically but not a spiritually "well watered" place. It is obvious that good, spiritual influences were slim to none in Sodom; considering the rainstorm of fire and brimstone that followed. His children did not turn out well. His wife gave herself to the city, forsook her children, and Lot's thinking became perverted as he was made willing to give his daughters away to a gang of perverts.

[Genesis 19:1—3] He still recognized the sight of heavenly things, but he had little use for them staying around. He must have known full well that this city was not a city for heavenly things. He knew the city would seek to pervert even heavenly things, since he had experienced such a perversion and corruption in his own life. His actions show us how he realized his living in such a place as Sodom was not a good decision. If it was not a good decision to make, then it was a good decision to keep. Yet, he had a hard time leaving his bad decision, as he passively fought to stay. [Gen 19:15, 16]

It is much like a person who comes to realize that it is not just other people who get lung cancer from years of smoking cigarettes, it has now happened to them. They ignored the warnings on the package. They even ignored the symptoms in their own body. Yet they refused to quit, even as their doctor tells them they only have months to live. It was a bad decision to start; it is a worse decision to keep.

NOTES TO LIVE BY: Note to self, ask GOD for wisdom and discernment every day.

Make sure all my plans are Biblical based, spiritually "well-watered," and bathed in prayer, with Christ and eternity in focus.

CHAPTER NINE
The common denominator

Abraham and Isaac: [Genesis 22:1—11]

Even as I am writing this book, I realize that it is most likely incomplete. Certainly our subject about making decisions is not exhausted in this version. Yet I present it as I have, because I believe it is a very important subject regarding the success of the family, the marriage, the church, and any other important subject one might mention. If some portion of this book is a help, a warning, or encouragement in someone's decision making, Praise God.

As I have stated before, as you study the Bible, you will begin to see a pattern develop as to when and how people make bad decisions in their lives. There is a common thread or denominator with bad decisions that I have found while doing this study.

When a decision is made in haste and without the right Biblical understanding, or in rejection or opposition to, the Word of God, there WILL BE terrible results, even though it may take many years to materialize or manifest. For instance, you can practice doing marriage or raising children by using your own philosophy for 10 to 20 years, and it might only take a second to discover it was wrong because it was not done the way God said to do it.

God asked Abraham to do something to Isaac that seems beyond our comprehension. How in the world could Abraham prepare to do such a thing as this? How is he to give God a sacrifice of his own son? To the average person this would seem like the right place to question God's thinking?

It seemed to be an unreasonable and bizarre request and looked like a good time to get further clarification on the plan. That was the perfect scenario to arrange for a substitute plan and call it obedience. There is no way that God would expect Abraham to do such a thing.

Look a little closer at just what Abraham was facing.

God asked Abraham to take the life of his son. Even though God stopped Abraham in the end, God still had Abraham go through the range of emotions or boundaries of mental anguish required in making such a determination as Abraham made.

Abraham's decision to make a sacrifice of his son was only right because it was what God said to do. There was really no other decision to be made. God told him to do this, and he felt he had no other choice but to obey. His obedience said much about who Abraham was, just as our obedience to God and His plan, and His program, which are contained in the Word of God, will say much about who we are as well. There is no room for reasoning.

That is the way we are to look at the commands of God. We must simply obey without reasoning.

What Abraham was asked to do must have been a VERY hard thing to do. It was a decision which required *enormous* faith in the God of the impossible. It was a decision that was *beyond* Abraham. It must have required a heavenly strength that is inconceivable. Abraham could not believe in himself more than he believed in God. He had to trust God whole heartily.

Discernment & Decision Making

We cannot believe in our abilities and / or trust our thinking more than we believe and trust in GOD.

When God asked for Isaac to be sacrificed, God asked for a piece of Abraham. Abraham could not think too long, or evaluate his loss too much, but he did need to determine to allow God to take part of him.

We must determine to lose part of ourselves when making Godly decisions that require us to lessen ourselves.

Abraham must have believed that God had a good reason to ask what He was asking Abraham to do. God would not do something frivolous, or unnecessary, but rather God always has a plan. His methods of execution must not be questioned.

We must accept God's working in our lives without questioning why, so that we can fulfill the work of God.

In short, we could conclude, after reading Genesis 22, that every decision we make, whether it is following the expressed, written Word of God, or it is following the principles of God's Word, must be made in faith, without questioning. We must find reason for God but not against Him.

RE'ASON, v.t.1. To examine or discuss by arguments; to debate or discuss.

Noah Webster's 1828 Dictionary

Reasoning against God is most often accompanied by doubt. Doubt is looking for proof. Proof is arranged for the flesh. The flesh is contrary to the Spirit. As Christians we are to live by faith. By faith is how we will please God, and it is the ONLY way to please Him.

The Christian life is a life to be lived by faith. We cannot see God, and we are to believe all that He has told us, or communicated to us, by and through His Word. By receiving His Word we are given His Spirit. His Spirit in us will connect us to the Word God has given to us. They go together. They complement one another.

Genesis 22:12 "And he said, Lay not thine hand upon the lad, neither do thou any thing unto him: for now I know that thou fearest God, seeing thou hast not withheld thy son, thine only son from me."

The blessings of God will follow obedience to God.

CHAPTER TEN
Make up your mind early

They say "All is well that ends well"

Joseph and Potiphar's wife: [Genesis 39:1—20]

It is best that we start connecting our children to God and His authority and His Word at a very early age, so that as they grow up, and branch out on their own, they will already be connected to God. As a result, they will not be as apt to lean to their own understanding when faced with decisions in their life. This will protect them from many bad decisions that most people make, once they get out on their own and feel the unrestrained power of making their own decisions.

Joseph and Mrs. Potiphar both made decisions that would seem to cost each of them dearly. However, there is a grand difference between these two people. I want us to look at behind the scenes of the decisions they each made.

[Genesis 37:4, 5] At an early age Joseph had already begun to realize that God was going to do great things in and through his life. He had very special dreams that alerted him to the favor that God would extend to him. Yet when he opened his month in immaturity he became envied and hated.

[Genesis 37: 12—14] Joseph must have learned early in his life to make decisions in obedience to authority no matter the cost to him personally. He listened to his father, did what he was told, and I would imagine this would seem to be a legacy passed down through the generations starting with his great grandfather Abraham. [Genesis 18:17—19]

Our family devotions on Ephesians 6 and Hebrews 12 are not merely so our children will obey us, but we encourage them to obey all authority that God gives to them in life. Ultimately we are teaching them to obey God.

Obedience is a legacy that is, or can be, passed down from generation to generation. We are responsible for teaching our children to obey, by word and by deed, so that one day our children will follow our good example as we obey God in all things and with all decisions, both great and small.

As we come to know the Word of God more intimately, by hiding it in our heart, IT can influence every decision we make.

Hebrews 4:12 "For the word of God *is* quick, and powerful, and sharper than any twoedged sword, piercing even to the dividing asunder of soul and spirit, and of the joints and marrow, and *is* a discerner of the thoughts and intents of the heart."

Our children are watching and they are listening.

Righteousness would be the compass of Joseph's life. No matter what others might do, or how they might behave themselves, Joseph sought righteousness. His desire was to please God in all things. In obedience he would maintain favor with God. In obedience he found and lived by the key to life.

Favor God, and God will favor you: Deuteronomy 30:15-21

[Genesis 37:23—28] Joseph was sold into slavery at the hand of his own brothers, after coming to check on his brothers, as his father had told him to do. He got in trouble while obeying. While obediently serving Potiphar and his household, Joseph was lied about in the commission of faithfully doing his job. He was put in prison in spite of doing right.

All the while he might have been thinking,
"When does the dream for my life come true?"

[Genesis 40:23] As he was in the prison, he was forgotten. He had interpreted a good dream regarding the butler, and yet the butler forgot him when he got out of prison. {Not to worry; God is in charge or remembering, so just make righteous decisions. God never forgets.} [Esther 6:1-3]

If you were to judge Joseph's life in the pit of rejection as his brothers sold him into slavery, or if you were to see him demoted after exhibiting the highest amount of character, or as you see him in the prison house, you might say life is not fair, so why do right. You might believe that good guys indeed finish hopelessly last. You might conclude that there is no justice so what difference does it make what I do. I would say you are hasty with your evaluation and judgment. We must give time for God to work His plan. These Biblical stories help us see the long-term effects.

On the other hand, what did it cost Potiphar and his wife?

His right decision was followed up by her bad decision, which would cost Joseph some time in prison for making the right decision. Her decision was made in lust and greed. Her decision was deceitful and crooked. When she could not get what she wanted, she decided to take what she wanted by force, using her position to lord over Joseph.

'You have made your bed, now sleep in it'

Her decision most likely cost her and her family mounds of trouble and serious setbacks. Their blessings went right out the window when Joseph went to prison. God promised blessings to those who blessed His people and cursing to those who cursed His people. What do you suppose happened to the Potiphars?

As we see this story in the Bible, it might seem that nothing happened to Mrs. Potiphar. She makes a bad decision, then she lied, and it seems like she gets away with it, but rest assured, she did not. You might ask how I know. Well, her story ends, and Joseph's story continues and has a great ending, and evil doers shall soon be cut down as the grass. [Psalm 37:1-11; 73:16-20, 27] The meek shall inherit the earth. However, you really do not want the earth in its present, run-down condition. It would be better to wait until it is made new again. Right now you would just be getting a fixer-upper.

That is why I said that you can judge and conclude a matter far too soon. Her story expires like bad milk spoiled by sitting in a desert sun too long. But Joseph's story goes forward in triumph and greatness, along with his entire family. [Genesis 41:37—44] They will become a great nation, but what happened to the Potiphars?

Discernment & Decision Making

You will most likely have to make decisions in life that will cost you something. You may suffer setbacks because you make right decisions. You may lose friendships and family, or you may have to quit a job to do right. You may lose much in the course of doing right. Yet we must always remember that if God is our life, we will always have life, so long as God is alive. That is the good news.

Joseph did not look or focus on what this would cost him personally. We do not hear murmuring or complaining from his life. In comparison, when we look at the story of Lot, we can conclude he should have considered the cost of moving his family to Sodom. In Joseph's situation he chose to do right irrespective of what it would cost him. Lot needed to do right irrespective of what he might have had to give up.

[Genesis 50:15—21] God can even make the wrong decisions that others make regarding our life turn out for the best, as we look to God to manage our life. All is well that ends well; **when** you make right decisions, you can count on it.

Favor God, and God will favor you: Deuteronomy 30:15-21

NOTES TO LIVE BY: Note to self, ask GOD for wisdom and discernment every day.

Make sure all my plans are Biblical based, spiritually "well-watered," and bathed in prayer, with Christ and eternity in focus.

If I favor God, then God will favor me: Deuteronomy 30:15-21

CHAPTER ELEVEN
Sentiment over substance

There are different types of decisions that people make. These can be summed up in two main headings. There are sentimental decisions and those that have substance. A sentimental decision might be presented as flashy and colorful, but often the good part of the experience is short-lived. It might make you temporarily feel better, but it will not last. On the other hand, a decision that has substance might not have the glitter of a sentimental decision, but it will usually fruitfully blossom and be long-lasting.

There are many stories in the Bible which could illustrate a sentimental type decision, but the story of Aaron and the making of the golden calf is plain and to the point.

Aaron built a golden calf for "*worship*" [Exodus 32:1-7]

Aaron was pressed and persuaded to disobey as he followed the dictates, whims, wishes, and schemes of wicked people in his care. He corrupted his charge, forsook his training, and trampled his God-given post, by giving the people what they wanted instead of what they needed. They needed to hear, "No!"

Moses is up in the mount, meeting with his Holy and righteous God, who was kind and gracious enough to deliver these people from the cruelty of their bondage. God was the one who appointed Aaron as the *first* High Priest, and this is the way Aaron and these people chose to repay GOD for His goodness? [1 Samuel 2:27-30]

He gave them their freedom, their liberty, their life, but instead of worshipping God, and living thankfully, they are found worshipping a *golden calf*? This was done under the leadership of Aaron, who had been commissioned by God as Moses' right hand man. What a bad testimony, and what a terrible decision! It was a dishonorable insult to Almighty God.

[Exodus 32:21—24] I like what Moses says: "What did this people unto thee..."

Aaron acts as if he was a reluctant and unwilling participant who had little to do with anything, according to him. He is almost an *innocent* by-stander according to him. He was nearly perfect and blameless except for tripping and accidentally throwing gold into the fire. Other than that, he really did not do anything. "I threw some gold into a fireplace and 'waa la,' out came a brand new golden calf!"

[V3—5] He *told* them what to do, *received* the gold from their hands, *fashioned* the gold with a graving tool, as he *made* and *shaped* the golden calf. He then *proclaimed* it as a god, *gave* it credit for delivering them from the enemy, *built* an altar, or a barbeque pit before it, and then attached a feast to the LORD to it and yet, Aaron practically had nothing to do with what those people did. He was pressured and persuaded to follow those he was supposed to lead.

After Moses told Aaron he had "brought so great a sin upon them," his only response was, "thou knowest the people." "The people" seem to get the blame, just as they did when Saul collected the bleating sheep and wicked king Agag. [1 Samuel 15:10—23]

Discernment & Decision Making

There was a pattern of rebellion and disobedience that developed with regards to Saul. He made a habit of blaming others. He acted as if he believed they were responsible for his misconduct and sinfulness. He proclaimed he was innocent and without responsibility. He inferred he wanted to do right, but others would not let him. When listening to Saul's denial of disobedience, he actually sounds convinced that he did nothing wrong. Saul seems bewitched, or charmed, as if a *spell* had been cast upon him. Maybe a spell was cast by the devil; we know rebellion is as the sin of witchcraft.

Rebellion is not so much that a person does what they want to do as much as it is a matter of not doing what they **know** they are supposed to do. That type of obvious, willful, arrogant, defiant disobedience, gives permission to the devil so that he may gain entry into a person's life. They are not resisting his influence, therefore they are welcoming him.

That seems to be what Saul did, and in so doing, he most likely came to believe he had not done anything wrong. From that time forward there was an *evil spirit* from the LORD that troubled Saul. He began to think the world was against him. He lived out his life a victim of a grand conspiracy which he alone was fueling.

[1Samuel 16:14, 15, 16, 23; 18:10; 19: 9] He became paranoid and delusional, believing David was his enemy. As you read his story, you will find that he began to think his family was against him as well. His symptoms were much like the very indicators that can be found with many people today, who are diagnosed as paranoid, delusional and schizophrenic. I wonder if most all such cases could be traced back to pure rebellion. Please remember that type of doctor prescribe pills, not solutions.

Saul seemed to be driven by a sentimental, idealistic heart. His passion and / or feelings seemed to be urging him forward in his quest. **It was not a matter of right or wrong, to him, as much as it was a matter of what he wanted to do**. [1Sam 13:8—13]

SEN'TIMENT, n. [from L. sentio , to feel, perceive or think.] 1. Properly. a thought prompted by passion or feeling. 2. In a popular sense, Thought; opinion; notion; judgment; the decision of the mind formed by deliberation or reasoning. Thus in deliberative bodies, every man has the privilege of delivering his sentiments upon questions, motions and bills. 3. The sense, thought or opinion contained in words, but considered as distinct from them. We may like the sentiment, when we dislike the language. 4. Sensibility; feeling.

IDE'AL, a. Existing in idea; intellectual; mental; as ideal knowledge. There will always be a wide interval between practical and ideal excellence. 1. Visionary; existing in fancy or imagination only; as ideal good. 2. That considers ideas as images, phantasms, or forms in the mind; as the ideal theory or philosophy.

IDE'ALISM, n. The system or theory that makes every thing to consist in ideas, and denies the existence of material bodies.

Noah Webster's 1828 Dictionary

Many people live very idealistic and sentimental lives.

Discernment & Decision Making

So many people have gone into debt buying and selling based on their emotions and feelings which we all know can change in a moment depending on a change in conditions surrounding their life. We find people setting aside and forsaking responsibility for the whims and pleasures of this life that will fade in the sunset. They are driven by a passion of what they want or how they want things to be. Many times the type of people who think like that will then work very diligently to make the world look the way they want it to be.

While I was visiting Pasco, Washington, for the purpose of preaching a revival, I saw a bumper sticker on a van which read, "Create the world you want to see." What a messy world of chaos we have, as almost 7 billion people are working to do that very self-centered thing, and they did not learn it from a bumper sticker either.

Sentimental and idealistic thinkers make decisions in agreement with their feelings, thoughts and opinions. Their judgment comes from how they think things should be, according to how they perceive life, and then they work to "create" the world they want to live in. They are easily bothered or provoked by others who have their own ideal "creation," which they are working to accomplish, if they discover it is different than their own.

Many people are driven by sentiment, not substance

Therefore their decisions are sentimental and not substantive. They get in their mind the *ideal* way of how things should be done, according to them, and reality gets in the way. They are the type of people who will do wrong **if** they have good intentions for doing wrong, or an unreasonable hope that everything will turn out alright in the end simply because they want it to. *Or in other words,* the end justifies the means, to those who have a sentimental mindset.

Saul seemed to believe that he was right to sacrifice because he had a good reason to sacrifice, even as it was not his place, nor in his power, nor his duty to do sacrifice. Nonetheless, it was ok because sacrificing is a good thing.

It was right to do sacrifice, or it was right for a sacrifice to be done, but it was wrong for **him** to be the one to do it. So why should he be so anxious to do a sacrifice, which is for God, when it was wrong for him to do it? The right he hoped to achieve is cancelled by the wrong he did in order to accomplish it.

We hear people make excuses all the time: "My kids like this or that" **or** "everybody else is doing it" **or** "we don't see the harm in doing it" **or** "it is just a kids movie" **and** "it is just for a little while" **or** "it is just one Sunday" **or** "as long as we get the job done, what difference does it make how we get the job done." This list could easily be extended.

There are all kinds of excuses, and / or permissions that people come up with, or make up, in order to do wrong and call it right. Then there are those who do wrong and blame someone else for their wrong. They do not see the harm in it. They act as if they do not know what is wrong with doing whatever they want to do. Furthermore, they want to do it, whether it is wrong or right. They certainly do not want someone telling they are wrong or why they are wrong. They do not want to know, and it would not likely make any difference if they did. They do not seem to think about or fear the consequence of wrong. They fear not

getting to do what they want more than they
fear God.

> 1 Samuel 15:22 "And Samuel said, Hath the LORD
> *as great* delight in burnt offerings and sacrifices, as
> in obeying the voice of the LORD? Behold, to
> obey *is* better than sacrifice, *and* to
> hearken than the fat of rams."

God says obedience is better than sacrifice, and
many a man lives as if sacrifice is better than obedience.
Disobedience is a key issue. Disobedience is a real
problem in many people's lives. Like the *spellbound denial*
of Saul, they do not consider they have disobeyed. They
hope to have God accept them in the end for their good
works even though God has told man in His Word He
never will.

Once a person has developed a sentimental
attachment to an idealistic lifestyle, whether it is self-made
or passed down through the family, it becomes very
difficult to detach from, even after a person is born-again. It
might just be in an area of their life where their conduct
and behavior seems yet unconverted, transformed or
renewed. [Romans 12:1, 2]

This is where we find Aaron and the people, looking
back to Egypt for the answers to living. They were looking
for a god to whom they could give credit to for the
goodness they experienced. They chose a god who was
very familiar to them. It was one to whom they already had
a sentimental affection toward.

> Joshua 24:14 "Now therefore fear the LORD, and
> serve him in sincerity and in truth: and **put away
> the gods which your fathers served on the other**

side of the flood, and in Egypt; and serve ye the LORD. 15 And if it seem evil unto you to serve the LORD, choose you this day whom ye will serve; whether the gods which your fathers served that *were* on the other side of the flood, or the gods of the Amorites, in whose land ye dwell: but as for me and my house, we will serve the LORD."

They made the golden calf because they still had a sentimental attachment to Egypt and its gods. Those gods heard not and could never help them. All that mattered to them at the time was what they thought they had. The God of heaven had delivered them and conquered the gods of the Egyptians, proving the God of heaven is more powerful. That did not matter, `sentiment won out over substance`.

It did not matter if God's way had been proven right; it was a matter of what they wanted for their lives. They chose the *golden calf* they could see instead of the God they could not see. They felt they could trust in what they could see, but they would not trust in what they could not see. They lived the "`except I shall see`..." doubting-Thomas life.

John 20:25 "The other disciples therefore said unto him, We have seen the Lord. But he said unto them, **Except I shall see** in his hands the print of the nails, and put my finger into the print of the nails, and thrust my hand into his side, **I will not believe.**"

The Hebrews thought because they were choosing a god they could see, they were choosing substance. Yet in reality they were choosing sentiment, over substance, as they chose to live by sight.

Discernment & Decision Making

Hebrews 11:1 "Now **faith is the substance** of things hoped for, the evidence of things not seen."

Sometimes, when cleaning out the attic or garage, we refuse to throw away things we have not used in years and probably will never use again, all for one very simple, and yet very complex reason. We like it. It has sentimental value to us. It may never materialize and become substance, but it will always be sentimental. {Just try and throw it away.}

The same is true with many *spiritual attics and garages* which contain things that we may use, but are nonetheless useless, and a waste of time. Yet we keep them for their sentimental value. {Many of these weights and besetting sins are from our old carnal life.} Are you guided by your idealistic way of how you think life should be? Are you making sentimental-type decisions for your life?

Proverbs 3: 5 "Trust in the LORD with all thine heart; and **lean not unto thine own understanding**. 6 In all thy ways acknowledge him, and he shall direct thy paths. 7 Be not wise in thine own eyes: fear the LORD, and depart from evil. 8 It shall be health to thy navel, and marrow to thy bones."

Aaron might have been a good second man, but he was not a good leader. When Moses was around, Aaron was good at following directions, but when Aaron was left alone, he was persuaded by the will of "the people," just as Pilate was.

Mark 15:15 "And *so* Pilate, **willing to content the people**, released Barabbas unto them, and delivered

Jesus, when he had scourged *him*, to be crucified." Luke 23:20 "Pilate therefore, willing to release Jesus, spake again to them."

By his actions, Pilate showed he was MORE willing to content guilty people than he was willing to release innocent Jesus. In so doing he exhibited that he feared the people more than he feared God. He was found looking for the "praises of man" instead of seeking the "praises of God." [John 5:44, 12:42, 43; 1 Corinthians 4:5]

We find Pilate, along with Saul and Aaron, believed that pleasing people was more important than pleasing God. Sacrifice was more important than obedience. These are just a few of the common denominators in these different stories.

This mentality is certainly very much a part of how many ministers go about decision making in their church. The main or major activities of the church, many times are designed according to the likes of the people, so that they will continue coming to church.

{This is the mentality Hybols and Olsten, along with thousands of church 'leaders' just like them, who have made church attendance acceptable to the masses; both to the saved and lost, who now enjoy coming to church. They consider their churches successful because of their **high** attendance. That is now the criteria of a successful 'church'. It is humanistic Christianity at its finest.}

There is likely that same tendency in everyone who has ever led people. It comes from a desire to be liked and a desire to be successful. That type of thinking creates a problem. If we want people to follow so badly that we are willing to set aside that which is right to achieve the praise of people, then we will sin and lead people to sin, in the process. [1 Kings 12:25-33]

Jeroboam led the people away from God and into sin.

1 Kings 12:26 "And Jeroboam said in his heart, Now shall the kingdom return to the house of David:"

One day there was a mob of people who came to a governor. They asked the governor to convict a Man they had determined as guilty. The governor examined the so-called guilty Man in all the areas where the wicked mob had said they found fault. The governor found no crime and declared the Man to be innocent and determined to beat Him and then let Him go free.

However, the bloodthirsty mob was not satisfied. They cried for blood. They shouted, "Crucify Him, Crucify Him." As the story goes, the governor decided to let the innocent Man be crucified, because he was willing to content, pacify, and quiet the angry mob. It was a very sinister and sentimental decision.

How many mothers and fathers give candy to their children if they will be quiet and with that act we have all unwittingly contributed to a hurtful philosophy which has caused us to only follow God **if** He gives us what we want? The determination of man is that God is only good when He gives us what we want, and God is bad when he does not. God is good when He lets us do what we want, and He is bad when He does not? **Man fails to see that God is good because of who He is and what He has** already **done.**

Good leaders are **not** made or determined by the treats they give. Good leaders are not led by people, popularity, or polls. Good leaders will not cater to people's whims in order to achieve likeability or popularity. Good leaders will be good leaders as they make decisions that follow God and His Word.

Bill Hybols rose to popularity and wrote an entire book describing how his pastorate is based in or upon giving people what they want so they will attend church. Yet the God he says he believes in describes that form of leadership as misguided and wicked. How can a leader in good conscience reconcile such decision making?

Do not make your decisions to please yourself by pleasing people; but make decisions that will please God and God alone. We must make decisions of substance, not sentimentalism.

> "Thou art worthy, O Lord, to receive glory and honour and power: for thou hast created all things, and **for thy pleasure** they are and were created." [Revelation 4:11]

CHAPTER TWELVE
Substance over sentiment

Hannah gave up her son as promised [1 Samuel 1:1-28]

Hannah made the opposite decision from the kind of decision that Aaron made. His decision was filled with sentimental value, and yet it had no substance. Therefore it was unprofitable.

> Exodus 32: 20 "And he took the calf which they had made, and burnt it in the fire, and ground it to powder, and strawed it upon the water, and made the children of Israel drink of it."

> Deuteronomy 9:21 "And I took your sin, the calf which ye had made, and burnt it with fire, and stamped it, and ground it very small, even until it was as small as dust: and I cast the dust thereof into the brook that descended out of the mount."

In the end, all of Aaron's labor and sweat went into a destructive decision. His work was destroyed because it was heavenly worthless. It only had hellish value. It may have been made of the most pure and precious gold available, but it was as valueless as any fool's gold. As with all waste, it went out into the draught of eternity.

Hannah made a decision that was filled with substance and void of sentiment. If we only knew the beginning of her story and not the end, we might consider her promise to God as purely wishful thinking and sentimental hogwash. It was not; it was full of substance.

She made a decision to live by faith, putting her trust in God. She was directed by a decision she made before she had to make a decision so that her decision was already made for her when she would be faced with a decision. Her decision was made before her son was born.

She made a decision, which became a commitment. It was made by faith, and it guided her life beyond what she could see. It would be good for each of us to follow her Godly example and make commitments before we are faced with decisions. These will be decisions to live by.

Let me explain by giving an example. If you will make the decision now to make a commitment that you will never watch another "R" rated movie, {all worldly movies for that matter}, then when you are confronted with the opportunity to watch a "R" rated movie, there will be no decision to make.

If you will make a decision now to make a commitment that you will never ride in a car with a member of the opposite sex, especially in your age bracket or younger, other than your spouse or children, then you will have no decision to make when confronted with such a decision to make.

If you will make a decision to make a commitment that you will tithe faithfully every week, no matter what bills come due, then when you are faced with such a decision to make, there will be no decision to make, for your decision will have been made already.

We could go on and on with decisions that we should commit to, presently, so that when we are faced with making a decision about these things later, there will be no decision to consider. We will have decided what to do before we are ever faced with such a decision. That will help protect us from making bad decisions.

This will be good for the home, the job, and the church.

In Samuel 15, we find Saul brought back the sheep.

[1 Samuel 15:1—23] God told him not to, but he did not obey. The Word of God was already in place to help protect and safeguard God's people. Yet when Saul found himself in a position of decision making, he decided wrongly, and thereby endangered himself and the people.

His decision was made for him;
therefore there was no decision to be made.

All he needed to do was accept that which was already decided and commit himself to the task of doing that which had been decided. There was no decision to make, only a commitment or covenant to follow. The matter was obviously not settled in Saul's heart. He made a decision on the run, and it cost him the kingdom and favor with God.

1 Samuel 1:11 "And she vowed a vow, and said, O LORD of hosts, if thou wilt indeed look on the affliction of thine handmaid, and remember me, and not forget thine handmaid, but wilt give unto thine handmaid a man child, then I will give him unto the LORD all the days of his life, and there shall no razor come upon his head."

[1 Samuel 2:20, 21] Hannah had made a commitment. It was an obligation that would guide her. It would settle her at the time when her emotions must have been higher as she brought Samuel to live with Eli. She was bound to keep her pledge. It turned out to be **in her best interest** as well as God's. Not only did it protect her when time came to fulfill the vow she had made, but she also received abundantly from her commitment to the LORD. **If you favor God with your life, then God will favor you**.

We need to make some decisions before we are confronted with those decisions, so that our decisions are made before we get there. That is a way of proper planning that will help protect you and safeguard your life and that of your family and church.

It will be in our best interest to make commitments now about things we do not really want to make decisions about later. As I mentioned before, there are some decisions God has already made for us, and therefore, there is really no decision to make. There is only a commitment to stick to and stand by. Therefore we should make our decision-commitments in light of God's principles, found throughout the Scriptures.

[Joshua 9:1—15] In Joshua chapter nine, we find the people of God made a very bad decision. When they made this decision they broke a covenant and commitment that was already in place. There was no good reason to allow themselves to be confronted with this decision. [Deuteronomy 7:1—6]

Decisions should never supersede commitments. That is why we should put commitments in place, much like a fence or wall that keeps undesirables from us. This will help keep us from making bad decisions. There was no decision for Joshua and the elders of Israel to make; God had made their decision for them.

They operated by putting sentiment before substance.

The Gibeonites would become a burden that would complicate Israel's life. Israel was forced to carry the burden of the Gibeonites into battle because **they used a decision to supersede a covenant** previously made. [Joshua 9:16—19, 10:1—7]

On the other hand, Hannah made an excellent decision; she took what she did not yet have, and made a Godly and selfless decision to give want she wanted to the LORD, before she had it, so that when she had it to give to the LORD, there would be no decision to make.

Hannah put substance before sentiment.

Instead of living by a decision, she actually lived by a commitment already made. What a great idea for living the Christ-like life; a life of commitment and substance is a life filled with value.

Hebrews 11:1 "Now **faith is the substance** of things hoped for, the evidence of things not seen."

These types of Godly commitments, not just decisions, but commitments, are made with the Word of God in mind. They will be some of the most long-lasting commitments you will ever make. **Is that not the case with the decision a person makes when they get married**? We must be sure to understand and teach marriage as a commitment, not a decision. It is a commitment to live selfless and peaceful with your spouse **for better or worse**. {There will be some of both.}

The reason we see so many separations, and divorces, is that people made decisions and not commitments. If we would look at decisions as commitments, we might be more cautious and careful about the decisions we make. **Somehow, decisions seem easier to get out of than covenants, contracts, and commitments.**

It is so good that God does not change His mind.

Malachi 3:6 "For I *am* the LORD, **I change not**; therefore ye sons of Jacob are not consumed."

James 1:17 "Every good gift and every perfect gift is from above, and cometh down from the Father of lights, with whom is no variableness, neither shadow of turning."

Romans 8: 35 "Who shall separate us from the love of Christ? shall tribulation, or distress, or persecution, or famine, or nakedness, or peril, or sword? 36 As it is written, For thy sake we are killed all the day long; we are accounted as sheep for the slaughter. 37 Nay, in all these things we are more than conquerors through him that loved us. 38 For I am persuaded, that neither death, nor life, nor angels, nor principalities, nor powers, nor things present, nor things to come, 39 Nor height, nor depth, nor any other creature, shall be able to separate us from the love of God, which is in Christ Jesus our Lord."

Ephesians 4:30 "And grieve not the holy Spirit of God, whereby ye are sealed unto the day of redemption."

Ephesians 1:13 "In whom ye also trusted, after that ye heard the word of truth, the gospel of your salvation: in whom also after that ye believed, ye were sealed with that holy Spirit of promise, 14 Which is the earnest of our inheritance until the redemption of the purchased possession, unto the praise of his glory."

Hebrews 13:8 "Jesus Christ the same yesterday, and to day, and for ever."

We can count on the decisions, commitments, covenants, and promises that God made regarding us. We can rejoice that our God is not fickle, or *wishy washy*, but He is steadfast, unrelenting, and always abounding. I am thankful for the promises of God and His determination to keep them.

God is great.

NOTES TO LIVE BY: Note to self, ask GOD for wisdom and discernment every day.

Make sure all my plans are Biblical based, spiritually "well-watered," and bathed in prayer, with Christ and eternity in focus.

If I favor God, then God will favor me: Deuteronomy 30:15-21

I need to have long term thinking in my decision making.

CHAPTER THIRTEEN
Buyer's remorse

David decided to stay home: 2 Samuel 11:1—11

When you make a decision to go shopping, it would be wise to have a budget and spending limit. When you go shopping, it would be best to only look at things you truly need. It would be wise not to wander about looking at things you will never be able to afford. Affordability is not determined by credit card limits. One afternoon of shopping, which has involved, or included, over-budget, impulse purchases, has put many a family into *budget bondage* for years and years to follow. Some purchases made in haste have taken a life time to pay back. Many people have ruined themselves financially for years to come by credit expenditures; just ask Washington DC.

One evening, in our first year of marriage, my wife and I went to look at a new car we had already set our heart upon. [James 1:14, 15] For weeks we thought about this vehicle and drove by the car lot looking at it again and again. One night we decided to stop by to take a closer look. We got out, saw the sales representative, drove the car, and we agreed to whatever the price so we could take it home. That night we sat at Red Robin eating, staring out the window, admiring our lovely new car. We were so proud and excited.

The next day, after I sobered up from my drunken stupor, {notice how close the spelling is to the word stupid}, I began to think about our decision. I certainly believe the Lord helped me sober up. I was facing a six hundred and fifty dollar a month payment. With that reality in mind, I looked out the window staring at that car. I did not admire it any longer, but rather abhorred my decision. I think they call it "**buyer's remorse**." [2 Samuel 13]

> 2 Samuel 13: 15 "Then Amnon hated her exceedingly; so that the hatred wherewith he hated her was greater than the love wherewith he had loved her. And Amnon said unto her, Arise, be gone."

> Matthew 27:3 "Then Judas, which had betrayed him, when he saw that he was condemned, repented himself, and brought again the thirty pieces of silver to the chief priests and elders, 4 Saying, I have sinned in that I have betrayed the innocent blood. And they said, What is that to us? see thou to that. 5 And he cast down the pieces of silver in the temple, and departed, and went and hanged himself."

Buyer's remorse; I had it, and I had it bad. It was a good thing to have at that point. It caused me to look for a way to take that car back. I picked up the phone, and I called a lawyer. He explained what to do, and I did it. I got our old car back. {It was not so old / there was nothing wrong with it / and I didn't need the new car.}. It was a good thing, too, because months later I surrendered to full-time Christian service, and a six-hundred-and-fifty-dollar-monthly-payment would possibly have hindered my decision or commitment to surrender.

The truth is that we do not always get a chance to take it back. We do not always get to know how much we will pay for the decision we are making at the outset. It might be fun on the ride home from the dealer, but in the morning, once the intoxication has worn off, and the pleasure is tempered by the cost we will pay for years to come, we might be stuck with what we have done, and cannot change it.

Many times when we make bad decisions, those decisions usually do not stand alone. We are prone to compound, complicate, and make issues worse by strengthening our resolve and determination in a bad decision. This is done with the hope of avoiding *facing the music.* In the process we commit a second offense, and maybe more, trying to cover up our wrong. Instead of admitting fault, taking the blame, and accepting the consequence; many times people will lie, cheat, and steal to get away from their bad decision. This is done with little to no regard with who else will get hurt in the process.

2 Samuel 11:1 "And it came to pass, after the year was expired, at the time when kings go forth to battle, that David sent Joab, and his servants with him, and all Israel; and they destroyed the children of Ammon, and besieged Rabbah. But David tarried still at Jerusalem."

With David, one bad decision to stay home from battle, led to a bad decision regarding Bathsheba, which led to another in an effort to cover up the first bad decision that should have never happened in the first place. He made matters worse farther down the wrong road he traveled. If David had been on the battlefield, Bathsheba would not have been invited over to the palace to meet David. If she had not been invited over, she would not have become pregnant with King David's illegitimate baby. If Bathsheba had not been pregnant, then David would not have had to plot and design the deliberate and vicious murder of a faithful soldier.

The illegitimate baby of David and Bathsheba died. The enemies of the LORD had cause to blaspheme, and David hurt his fellowship with the LORD. It all started *innocently* enough with two grown people who were old enough to make their **own decisions**. Yet **their decision** had a *domino effect* that brought danger and hurt to other people.

Your decisions most likely will **always** affect other people

It was a very costly decision for Uriah, Bathsheba, David, his children, and for the kingdom. David's bad decision brought about problems for other people, not just David. What started as one offense of staying at home, led to David and Bathsheba committing adultery, and it turned into many years of pain and sorrow from the *compound fracture* that rippled through David's family.

Numbers 14:18 "The LORD *is* longsuffering, and of great mercy, forgiving iniquity and transgression, and by no means clearing *the guilty*, visiting the iniquity of the fathers upon the children unto the third and fourth *generation*."

We could consider and study many stories in the Bible, and we should, where we find remorseful buyers. Judas regretted the deal he made with the devil and his own lust. He tried to return his decision of betrayal, threw the silver on the floor, but his conscience will haunt him throughout eternity. We could also consider the story of Esau who regretted trading his birthright for a bowl of soup. There was a no return policy on that soup. His belly he did fill, but his heritage was goodly empty.

Hebrews 12:16 "Lest there be any fornicator, or profane person, as Esau, who for one morsel of meat sold his birthright. 17 For ye know how that afterward, when he would have inherited the blessing, he was rejected: for he found no place of repentance, though he sought it carefully with tears."

Make sure you do not buy anything you cannot truly afford. Do not make a purchase that will take a life-time to repay. Do not keep a sinful life that will take an eternity to pay back. Lastly, remember that Jesus redeemed it all.

No standing in line when asking Jesus to take your returns.

1 John 1:9 "If we confess our sins, he is faithful and just to forgive us *our* sins, and to cleanse us from all unrighteousness."

[See also the story found in Joshua 9]

Discernment & Decision Making

NOTES TO LIVE BY: Note to self, ask GOD for wisdom and discernment every day.

Make sure all my plans are Biblical based, spiritually "well-watered," and bathed in prayer, with Christ and eternity in focus.

If I favor God, then God will favor me: Deuteronomy 30:15-21

I need to have long term thinking in my decision making.

Bad decision will ripple through my life, so I must be careful not to make decisions I will regret.

CHAPTER FOURTEEN
It will not work without application

Solomon knew what to do [1 Kings 3:5—15]

Deuteronomy 30:11 "For this commandment which I command thee this day, **it is not hidden from thee**, neither is it far off. 12 It is not in heaven, that thou shouldest say, Who shall go up for us to heaven, and bring it unto us, that we may hear it, and do it? 13 Neither is it beyond the sea, that thou shouldest say, Who shall go over the sea for us, and bring it unto us, that we may hear it, and do it? 14 **But the word is very nigh unto thee, in thy mouth, and in thy heart, that thou mayest do it.**"

Once upon a time, I was told if you are in the mountains of California and you come across poison oak, if you look around, you will find a Manzanita tree. They say there is a special way to cook or prepare the Manzanita tea leaf which will help bring healing and relief to those who contract poison oak. Whether this is true or not, it is true that throughout nature you can find the cure close by the poison. The venom is treated with the anti-venom.

If you have knowledge you can have the cure, and the cure might be close by; but **no amount of cure can or will ever work if it is not applied**. The failure in having a cure available is the failure to apply the cure. Without application, it will not work, no matter how much of the cure is at your disposal. Application is key and essential to healing.

Notice that Solomon asked God for wisdom. God gave Solomon what he asked for, and God tells us all we have to do is ask, and God will give us wisdom too.

Discernment & Decision Making

James 1:5 "If any of you lack wisdom, **let him ask of God**, that giveth to all *men* liberally, and upbraideth not; and it shall be given him."

Solomon was granted wisdom from God *for* the purpose of leading God's people. He also was used of God for the purpose of contributing writings to Scripture. Solomon wrote Ecclesiastes, Song of Solomon, and Proverbs. He was used by God as one of the wisest men, if not the wisest to ever live. God shares this wisdom with us as He gives us a glimpse at a few decisions that came before Solomon. The Bible showcases for us the great discernment and wisdom used by Solomon.

One of the most famous can be found in 1 Kings 3:16-28

Wisdom solves problems.

In his wisdom Solomon determined that the real mother could be found by seeing which mother had the greatest love for the child in question. Solomon basically said, "Would the real mother please step forward and claim her baby."

Solomon was faced with a very tough decision. He had to decide which mother was the *momma* of the baby both women wanted to claim. He was not present the night before to be an eyewitness. There were no security cameras in their house to revisit what happened. He did not know these women personally. In the absence of personal knowledge he had to rely on wisdom from God.

What was he to do? He knew how the real momma would act. She would protect and nurture her baby at all cost. He also suspected that the false mother would not care for the welfare of the child in the same manner the child's real momma would. This determination was made in wisdom which Solomon received from God. God gave Solomon an understanding heart so he could know the ways of man.

To know the ways of man is to know how a man can protect himself not only from others, but he can know how to protect himself from himself. **The worse enemy that any man will face is himself**. It would be wise for man to come to the realization early in life and have the understanding that he has and will hurt himself more than anyone else could. Bad decisions will have an adverse or *enemy effect* on our lives.

Solomon is a perfect example of this truth. He had inherited a great kingdom. He had received protection from his enemies. He had great wealth and riches. He had all the wisdom that any man could ever have. He knew the *pitfalls* of man. He saw all the *booby traps* of life. He knew the destructive and corrupting measures the devil will use to tempt a man. Yet, even though Solomon possessed the greatest wisdom known to man, he still failed God and himself, by making decisions when he knew better.

All throughout the book of Proverbs, Solomon warns his son to beware of the strange woman who flatters with her lips.

Proverbs 5:3 "For the lips of a strange woman drop as an honeycomb, and her mouth is smoother than oil:" [Proverbs 2:16; 6:24; 7:1—27]

However, in the end, Solomon did not do what he knew was right to do. He did what he knew not to do, and in so doing Solomon hurt himself more than anyone else could have, because he failed to **use** the wisdom he possessed. He failed as he departed from his own good, sound, God-given, and inspired advice.

> James 4:17 "Therefore to him that knoweth to do good, and doeth *it* not, to him it is sin."

Wisdom is not for looks but for use [1 Kings 11:1—11]

It is not simply good enough to know better and to instruct others to do right; it is most important that our lives become a walking testimony of Godly wisdom. We must not become castaways because we stop living by the statues which we have learned and instructed others to live by.

> 1 Timothy 4:16 "Take heed unto thyself, and unto the doctrine; continue in them: for in doing this thou shalt both save thyself, and them that hear thee."

Even if a man should become a castaway, by living a sinful life in opposition to Godly living he taught others to live by, that does not make wisdom and Godly living wrong. **Truth and wisdom are always right no matter what we do with them**. Truth is always truth and wisdom is always wisdom, and they are not changed by what we do to the contrary. We might become a castaway, but wisdom and truth never will.

It is also important to remember that decisions we make can have a long-lasting effect on our lives and the lives of those under our influence. For that reason we must let God direct our paths. [Proverbs 3:5, 6] God can see the future we cannot see, and therefore we must consult God and do as He says, with each step we take. We must not take steps contrary to His Word.

Solomon hurt his family long-term because of what he did. In fact the entire kingdom would suffer the effects of Solomon's sin for years and years to come. Who is going to deconstruct the temples he had built to other gods? If wise Solomon did it, then it must be right; right?

This should be a sobering thought for us as parents and leaders. How will our decisions affect the lives of the generations which will follow us? Will our descendants suffer for our wrong, unto the third and fourth generation?

Exodus 20:5 "Thou shalt not bow down thyself to them, nor serve them: for I the LORD thy God *am* a jealous God, visiting the iniquity of the fathers upon the children unto the third and fourth *generation* of them that hate me;"

Exodus 34:7 "Keeping mercy for thousands, forgiving iniquity and transgression and sin, and that will by no means clear *the guilty*; visiting the iniquity of the fathers upon the children, and upon the children's children, unto the third and to the fourth *generation*."

Numbers 14:18 "The LORD *is* longsuffering, and of great mercy, forgiving iniquity and transgression, and by no means clearing [the guilty], visiting the iniquity of the fathers upon the children unto the third and fourth *generation*."

Deuteronomy 5:9 "Thou shalt not bow down thyself unto them, nor serve them: for I the LORD thy God *am* a jealous God, visiting the iniquity of the fathers upon the children unto the third and fourth *generation* of them that hate me,"

Are we asking God for wisdom and discernment? It is there for the asking. God has made wisdom, the Holy Spirit, Godly counselors, the Bible and prayer abundantly available for our liberal use, but more importantly than availability and possession of wisdom, there is the necessary use which makes wisdom work for us. Are we accessing or using all of the avenues to wisdom and decision making that God has graciously made available to us? **It will not work** if **it is not applied**.

James 4:17 "Therefore to him that knoweth to do good, and doeth *it* not, to him **it is sin**."

CHAPTER FIFTEEN
Dangerous or tame?

1 Kings 13:1—19

There are many things in life which are very dangerous, even though they may appear to be harmless. To a child an electrical outlet might appear as harmless as a bubble gum machine. However, if they stick a dime into the empty slot of an electrical outlet like it is a bubble gum machine, they could be seriously hurt. The dime will not be received the same at both slots. The bubble gum machine will give a sweet surprise while the electrical outlet will give a shocking surprise. The one will bring a smile, the other a frown.

The king is dangerous and the old prophet is tame?

As I read the story of the young prophet from 1Kings 13, it is apparent that he determined that going home with the king would have been dangerous. Yet as the story continues, we find that he was persuaded to accept the offer of the older prophet. The young prophet believed the invitation from the old prophet was believable, tame, and harmless. He had no respect for the king, but he gave the old prophet reverence. The truth is that **the old prophet was just as dangerous** as the king because of, or in light of, God's Word. He made a *fatal* decision because he saw the dangerous as tame.

Just before I started writing this book, I was told a story about a woman in Pennsylvania who was killed by her pet bear. I will spare you many of the details and just share some pertinent highlights. The lady entered to feed the bear and clean its cage, as she had done numerous times before, when to her surprise she was attacked by her

109

pet. She had owned the bear about nine years. I am sure she expected no danger from the pet that she trusted to be tame.

[Judges 16:4-21] As you read the story of Samson from Judges 16, you will find that Samson had the same confidence with Delilah as the woman had with her pet bear. The lady who had a bear for a pet thought she controlled or managed such strength, and therefore underestimating the true danger. She believed there were common feelings and a friendly relationship between her and her pet bear. She determined the animal was trustworthy. In the same manner, Samson went to sleep on Delilah's lap, feeling safe and sound, thinking she was tame and trustworthy. He did not see her as dangerous.

Many people have kept unsaved friends around after getting saved because they believe these friendships are tame and safe. Many parents have allowed their children to have friendships with those of the world because they think they are harmless. Many people have flirted with great *unknown* danger, only to suffer the sorrow and pain that accompanies all sin. Sin is never trustworthy. That is why we must stay away from all appearance of evil. It might be more dangerous than it appears to be.

2 Corinthians 6:14 "Be ye not unequally yoked together with unbelievers: for what fellowship hath righteousness with unrighteousness? and what communion hath light with darkness? 15 And what concord hath Christ with Belial? or what part hath he that believeth with an infidel? 16 And what agreement hath the temple of God with idols? for ye are the temple of the living God; as God hath said, I will dwell in them, and walk in them; and I will be their God, and they shall be my people. 17

Discernment & Decision Making

Wherefore come out from among them, and be ye separate, saith the Lord, and touch not the unclean thing; and I will receive you, 18 And will be a Father unto you, and ye shall be my sons and daughters, saith the Lord Almighty."

Samson would have never laid down his head on the lap of some Philistine soldier, because he would have recognized the incredible danger associated with his *known* enemy. He had a proper amount of respect for the *known* enemy, which caused him to keep his distance from the Philistine soldiers. However, he did not have proper respect for Delilah the *unsuspected* enemy.

This is certainly true as we consider making a decision. Some decisions seem very tame and harmless. These are decisions which we make so quickly and easily. Yet many times we make these *easy and tame* decisions without proper consideration of accessible truth. We can make a very bad decision as we think only of the temporal and how this decision will presently affect us, and yet we fail to see the long term hurt of affecting ourselves or others. These decisions are made without considering God's perspective.

[Joshua 7:1—11] Israel made such a decision at Ai. The decision to go to Ai was made quick and easy. They did not see this decision as dangerous, but they saw it as tame. Unfortunately for them their decision was packed with unseen danger. It exploded right in their face, much like a firecracker would explode in the face of a little boy who got a short fuse and held on just a second too long. The little boy who only sees the fun and underestimates the danger of a firecracker, might be forced to live blind his entire life because at age seven he could not see the danger.

111

Discernment & Decision Making

[2 Samuel 13:1—29] Amnon decided to force himself upon his half-sister. He believed his decision was filled with peace and pleasure. Amnon certainly did not consider nor factor in his own death when he received instructions from his *friend* Jonadab. At the time, Amnon receive this "good-friendly" advice, it seemed like great idea. It was a decision that served Amnon well even as it brought hurt and harm to others. His pleasure was short-lived. Once Amnon got what he wanted, his decision turned on him. What he thought would be a fulfilling pleasure, became disgusting to him after he got what he thought he wanted.

> 2 Samuel 13:15 "Then Amnon hated her exceedingly; so that the hatred wherewith he hated her was greater than the love wherewith he had loved her. And Amnon said unto her, Arise, be gone."

There are many similar stories in the Bible. At the point of decision making the decision seems tame and harmless. Yet in time, the truth is, these types of decisions are found to be filled with explosive danger.

How many stories have we heard about the child who is mauled by the family pit bull, as the child was playing peacefully in the yard? The people who owned the dog believed it was tame enough to be in the yard where the child was playing, in spite of the fact that we all have heard too many stories about children who have been mauled by the family pit bull. How do they now live with their horrible decision of underestimating the danger of such an animal?

It would seem we know about the danger, but many times we **choose** to ignore it.

Discernment & Decision Making

I am reminded of too many stories of pastors who made decisions which might have seemed innocent and harmless at the time, but in the end there were very negative results. There are stories of personal sin committed even though every pastor should understand and know the danger of the forbidden woman or the unwise counseling session that should never take place.

What about the decision of an error in judgment?

I am reminded of a story where a pastor made a decision which was to affect the life of one man and his wife. It became a decision that would affect the entire church. The man had done wrong. So the pastor hastily and quickly dealt with the man, without properly considering the rooting system of this man and his wife. The man certainly presented himself as a tare, but his roots were connected or intertwined with much wheat in that church.

The decision to remove such a man, at the time, seemed tame and yet it was a decision laced with great risk. As a result, the pastor underestimated the danger. His harsh handling of this matter, lead to the hurt of the entire church. What he thought would fix the problem actually became the dynamite that would explode the whole church. His good intentions mattered not. His years of service mattered little. When all was said and done, the pastor ended up having to leave in shame.

God might have tried to impart wisdom to the pastor at the time, but most likely, just like most of us, he did not, could not, or would not listen. Like Samson before him, he probably relied on his own strength, having confidence in the tameness of his decision making and seeing 'Delilah' as no threat whatsoever. Samson could have destroyed her with his little pinky, **if** he had seen her as dangerous.

Instead, he willingly laid down upon her knees in peace, after bearing his heart to her. She must have begun to stroke the hair of his head so gentle and tame-like, even though evil was determined in her heart. **What he would never have done on the battlefield, he did in the parlor**.

> The parlor game seemed so innocent. The playful flirtation seemed so genuine. The atmosphere seemed so calm and inviting as she gently stroked the hair of his head. She seemed so tame, and yet her heart was filled with a dangerous evil, but because he was unaware of it, he had no hope of escaping.

No one in their right mind gives their child to a known pervert child-molester. Yet I wonder how many thousands of children have been given to babysitters, uncles, teachers, coaches, priest, step-fathers and the like, who seemed to be so tame and trustworthy. I wonder how many parents have not properly considered the danger of a close family friend who ended up being a monster in the neighborhood. I wonder how many supposedly tame sleep-over and slumber parties have been filled with *unknown* and *unsuspected* danger which has affected many a child, emotionally and mentally, for the rest of their life.

How many countless souls will be in hell who did not consider the danger of rejecting Jesus Christ invitation of righteousness and salvation, believing that their own righteousness is tame and good enough to get them into heaven. [Romans 10:1-4] How wrong they are!

Proverbs 22:3 "A prudent man foreseeth the evil, and hideth himself: but the simple pass on, and are punished."

Are you living a tame or dangerous life?

To live a tame life, you must live daily by the Word of God. If you do not, then rest assured that you are living a very dangerous life.

Discernment & Decision Making

NOTES TO LIVE BY: Note to self, ask GOD for wisdom and discernment every day.

Make sure all my plans are Biblically based, spiritually "well-watered," and bathed in prayer, so that I keep Christ and eternity in focus.

If I favor God, then God will favor me: Deuteronomy 30:15-21. Obeying God will ensure a blessed life.

I need to have long term thinking in my decision making. I must not have knot-hole philosophy.

Bad decisions will ripple through my life, so I must be careful not to make decisions I will regret.

Ask God to help me see the dangerous in what appears to be tame. I must put on the whole armor or God, daily.

_____
_____
_____
_____
_____
_____
_____
_____
_____
_____
_____
_____

CHAPTER SIXTEEN
The decision of no decision
2 Samuel 13:1—23

Some people make decisions very quickly without thinking long enough about the decision they are about to make. Some will ask counsel to seek help with the decision that is before them. Yet, there are many people who have so much fear about making the wrong decision that they will not make a decision at all.

Tamar, the sister of Absalom, had been raped by her step-brother, Amnon. Then Amnon did further damage by abandoning her as though she were useless trash. When Absalom, Tamar's brother, found out about it, he was very wroth. His anger seemed to grow stronger because of the fact that when his father found out he did nothing about it.

It would seem David should have, but did not properly respond to an obvious injustice committed by one of his children against another. There was confusion and trouble because a decision should have been made but nothing was done. Since nothing was done, Absalom, after waiting two full years, decided to take matters into his own hands.

[Genesis 34:1—5, 13, 25—31] In another case, Jacob's sons should not have done what they did. They may not have liked the way their father handled the issue of Dinah, their sister, but a decision was made and everyone should have lived by the decision that was made by their father, Jacob.

There is a danger in not making the right decision. No one wants to be a failure. However there is just as much of a danger, if not more, in **not** making a decision because you are afraid of making the wrong decision.

There is such a fear of making a wrong decision which keeps many people from making a decision at all. There may be times when we do not need to do anything at all, and it is best to stay out of the way, but it is not good to not make a decision simply because we are scared to make a mistake.

There are many circumstances in life that call for a decision to be made. At these times, we must make a decision, in spite of the fact that we might fear it may turn out to be wrong. Would it not be better to fail by doing wrong, than to fail by doing nothing at all?

Proverbs 24:16 "For a just *man* falleth seven times, and riseth up again: but the wicked shall fall into mischief."

[Luke 19:20-23] I believe the Bible teaches that God gives mercy to those who have a heart to do right, even though they failed. I believe it also teaches that if we are trying to honor God by doing right and making decisions with God in mind, then He can and will extend great grace to us, even if our decision turns out badly.

The issue where Tamar was raped was a violation that needed a just response. Notice David's entire family suffered because of David's **in**action and failure to respond to an obvious breech that brought shame and harm, not just to Tamar, but also to the people of God.

Absalom sees the injustice, or lack of justice, as though Amnon got away with it. So Absalom chose to do wrong, trying to right a wrong that was unresolved. This brought turmoil into his life. It was not his decision to make. Absalom brought Amnon to his vengeful court of injustice. As a result, Amnon would never face his wrong with a chance to make it right because of Absalom's vengeance. David's non-decision contributed to Absalom's wrong behavior. The situation became more and more complicated because of **the decision of no decision**. Because David did not respond, Amnon died. Lawlessness will breed chaos. Praise God for those who protect and serve true justice. [Romans 13:1-6]

You have no decision if the decision is made.

Concerning the matter of Jacob's daughter Dinah who was violated by Shechem, in the eyes of Jacob's sons, {and maybe in our eyes as well}, justice was not served. However, whether the sons of Jacob felt justice was served or not, Jacob as the father dealt with the situation as he saw fit. Did he make the right decision?

> Deuteronomy 22:28 "If a man find a damsel that is a virgin, which is not betrothed, and lay hold on her, and lie with her, and they be found; 29 Then the man that lay with her shall give unto the damsel's father fifty shekels of silver, and she shall be his wife; because he hath humbled her, he may not put her away all his days." [Exodus 22:16-17]

Jacob made his decision without the benefit of this passage in Deuteronomy 22. It had not been written. Apparently Jacob responded right, in accordance with what we can now read in Scripture. Shechem's son had a chance to make it right. The matter was measured and decided by Jacob. It was his decision to make. Therefore the matter should have been considered settled.

Discernment & Decision Making

There are situations that will arise that will require making a decision. In these times, we must always seek God about what to do, or not to do. God has Alpha / Omega vision which gives Him the benefit of seeing from beginning to the end. He is the one to go to seeking answers to all questions about all things. He always knows what we should do, and when He tells us what to do by giving us peace about something, we must do what God has given us peace about. If we do not, we may cause more problems. Small issues that are unresolved can grow out of control very quickly. Little weeds are the easiest to remove.

What about when the Bible has already spoken specifically, or principally, on the matter in question? It has been eloquently stated that there should never be a question mark put where God has placed a period. Everything God has spoken is truth.

THE DECISION OF NO DECISION
is or can be a dangerous thing

CHAPTER SEVENTEEN
Righteousness over rightness

Romans 10: 1 "Brethren, my heart's desire and prayer to God for Israel is, that they might be saved. 2 For I bear them record that they have a zeal of God, but not according to knowledge. 3 For they being ignorant of God's righteousness, and going about to establish their own righteousness, have not submitted themselves unto the righteousness of God. 4 For Christ is the end of the law for righteousness to every one that believeth."

Paul knew what he was talking when he wrote this passage in Romans 10. Before this conversation he had killed many Christians believing he was doing the will of God. I wonder how many times we do things wrong in the name of God?

Genesis 3:5 "For God doth know that in the day ye eat thereof, then your eyes shall be opened, and ye shall be as gods, knowing good and evil."

Ever since the end of the garden days, when man first partook of the forbidden tree, man became his own 'god' knowing good and evil. Even though we are saved, the issue of being right is still very much a part of our existence. Which of us is content to leave an argument or debate without being the one to say the last word? It is all part of our desire to be right, or the fear of having others see us as wrong. We are not so accepting of opposing views that could disrupt what we want to be true.

My mind is made up so no one should try to change it.

We make the same point over and over so we can be right. It is rare that we change the opinion of the other person because they too feel they need to be right. During a debate, even if we come to realize that we might be somewhat wrong, we continue to make a point, so we can partially be right. Who wants to be guilty of wrong and then admitting it; how painful is that? If we are found to be wrong, we can still proclaim our good intention of trying to be right, to save face. That usually will make it less painful.

Would you want to know you are wrong if you are?

I was at a church one afternoon when the pastor asked an associate to fill the baptistery for a baptism to be conducted the following evening. He explained that he wanted to baptize that night, but there would not be sufficient time to heat the water. Therefore he asked his associate to fill it and heat the water so it would be ready for the following night. The associate said that he could fill the baptistery and heat the water before the evening service, that same day. The pastor knew that was not possible and told the associate the same. The associate argued and stated that he was convinced it could be filled and heated by the evening service. The two disagreed, but in his wisdom the pastor decided to let the associate discover he was wrong in time.

The associate decided not to leave things to chance. Instead of just filling the baptistery and allowing the heater to do the work, he worked to heat water and carried it to the baptistery in an effort to prove he was right. He toted pan after pan from the kitchen downstairs, up to the auditorium. This process of *heat and carry* took better than a few hours.

Just before the service the associate assured the pastor the water was warm and ready. After the baptisms, that evening, the pastor asked the associate and those who were baptized how warm the water was. He received two very different answers. Those baptized said it was cold, but surprisingly enough the associate said it was *ok*. The pastor told his associate that the people who were baptized said it was cold. The associate replied it was *somewhat* warm. He refused to be wrong, because he so believed he could be right. He had good intentions.

Deuteronomy 12:8 "Ye shall not do after all *the things* that we do here this day, every man whatsoever *is* **right in his own eyes**."

Judges 17:6 "In those days *there was* no king in Israel, *but* every man did *that which was* **right in his own eyes**."

Judges 21:25 "In those days *there was* no king in Israel: every man did *that which was* **right in his own eyes**."

Proverbs 14:12 "There is a way which seemeth right unto a man, but the end thereof are the ways of death."

I shall be right no matter who gets hurt.

[2 Samuel 2:18-23; 3:17-27] Abner killed Asahel in battle. Asahel died because he was determined to be right and refused the wise counsel of Abner. Then Abner came to set things right. He sought to reunite the divided kingdom to David. When Joab found out that Abner had come to see David, and he let Abner leave in peace, he became very upset with King David. Then Joab sent to fetch Abner and bring him back to Hebron under false pretenses, so he could have opportunity to kill Abner. He then killed Abner to avenge the death of his brother Asahel. [2 Samuel 3:24, 25] When he was confronted, he tried to proclaim his own righteousness; but really he just wanted to be right.

> 2Samuel 3:27 "And when Abner was returned to Hebron, Joab took him aside in the gate to speak with him quietly, and smote him there under the fifth rib, that he died, for the blood of Asahel his brother."

He was right in his own eyes, but he certainly was not righteous before God. He endangered the kingdom's harmony and brought potential hurt and harm to God's cause of peace. **Joab chose rightness over righteousness**. He would prove he was right, even though he was not righteous.

Let us arm wrestle to decide who is right.

> [2 Samuel 24:1-4] 4 "Notwithstanding the king's word prevailed against Joab, and against the captains of the host". And Joab and the captains of the host went out from the presence of the king, to number the people of Israel."

David told Joab to number the people. Joab argued the point realizing this was the wrong course of action, but the Bible tells us that David "prevailed." It would seem that David got in the last word. David got what he wanted. Or did he? Many times we just think we get what we want.

The point might have seemed arguable, as arguments often do, but it was not. David felt he was right, and Joab believed he was right. There was a disagreement. Both men could not be right. There was a test of wills. Well, as it turned out, David was "right", in his own eyes, and he prevailed, but he was not righteous. [2 Samuel 24:10-15] God declared him unrighteous. David's unrighteous decision brought hurt and harm to thousands of lives. Some seventy thousand people died so David could be right. We shall find that rightness is not good enough, but righteousness is the best standard by which we should strive to live.

Do you only seek counsel from those who will agree with you, or will you allow some to challenge your thinking?

1Kings 22: 5 "And Jehoshaphat said unto the king of Israel, Enquire, I pray thee, at the word of the LORD to day. 6 Then the king of Israel gathered the prophets together, about four hundred men, and said unto them, Shall I go against Ramothgilead to battle, or shall I forbear? And they said, Go up; for the Lord shall deliver it into the hand of the king. 7 And Jehoshaphat said, Is there not here a prophet of the LORD besides, that we might enquire of him? 8 And the king of Israel said unto Jehoshaphat, There is yet one man, Micaiah the son of Imlah, by whom we may enquire of the LORD: but I hate him; for he doth not prophesy good concerning me, but evil. And Jehoshaphat said, Let not the king say so."

Here we find the matter of King Ahab. He had a battle to fight, but he did not want to fight it alone. So he invited Jehoshaphat to join him. Jehoshaphat agreed, but first he wanted to know if Ahab had inquired of the LORD regarding the battle. Ahab *then* called 400 prophets whom he knew would speak favorably about what he intended to do. Jehoshaphat wondered if there was not a prophet who disagreed with Ahab's call to fight. There was, but Ahab had not called him to speak because he hated him. He hated the prophet Micaiah because he never agreed with Ahab. King Ahab needed to be right. He could not have anyone disagree with him. Naboth had disagreed with King Ahab, and it cost him his life. Ahab had a desire to be right, but he had no desire to be righteous.

So Ahab was fine to go forward based on information from 400 agreeable prophets. The thought that they agreed with him gave him a false peace. [V13, 14] They secured him in his rightness. Those who dare challenge the rightness of his position would meet the fury of disagreeing with Ahab the king. He then makes the statement of triumph:

> 1 Kings 22:27 "And say, Thus saith the king, Put this fellow in the prison, and feed him with bread of affliction and with water of affliction, **until I come in peace**. 28 And Micaiah said, If thou return at all in peace, the LORD hath not spoken by me. And he said, Hearken, O people, every one of you."

Ahab did not return in peace. Miciah had told the king the truth. He was in fact the only prophet who told King Ahab the truth. If the king had been **more** interested in truth and righteousness than he was in being right, he would have skipped the battle, stayed home, and lived to die another day.

Ahab is not unlike most people. People generally surround themselves with people who agree with them. They only seek advice from those who they know will agree with them. If they should get counsel from someone else, it is only for agreement, and they will disregard any counsel that disagrees with them. They do this to their own hurt.

> Proverbs 12:15 "The way of the fool is right in his own eyes: but he that hearkeneth unto counsel is wise."

Rightness is one of man's biggest problems. It is rooted in man's pride. The devil works in the darkness and deception of man's *rightness*. When man deals in rightness instead of righteousness he fails himself, others and most importantly, he fails God. When a person has such a strong desire to be right <u>at all cost</u>, the desire to be right is elevated, and righteousness is devalued in the process.

[1 Kings 22:29-40] Ahab dressed up in a costume cleverly cloaked in his rightness; but he still died foolishly in unrighteousness. How many billions of people live life cloaked in their own unrighteousness who will die right in their own eyes?

In 1 Kings 12, we find that Rehoboam was approached by the congregation of Israel saying,

> 4 "Thy father made our yoke grievous: now therefore make thou the grievous service of thy father, and his heavy yoke which he put upon us, lighter, and we will serve thee."

Rehoboam told them to depart and return in three days, and he would give them an answer. First, Rehoboam "consulted with the old men," who "stood before Solomon." Those gray-headed men had experience and spoke from a position of wisdom having served his father.

7 "And they spake unto him, saying, If thou wilt be a servant unto this people this day, and wilt serve them, and answer them, and speak good words to them, then they will be thy servants for ever. 8 But he forsook the counsel of the old men, which they had given him, and consulted with the young men that were grown up with him, and which stood before him:"

Rehoboam did not like the counsel of the old men. That is because he already had his mind made up. He declared he was "right," and all he was looking for was someone to agree with him.

9 "And he said unto them, What counsel give ye that we may answer this people, who have spoken to me, saying, Make the yoke which thy father did put upon us lighter? 10 And the young men that were grown up with him spake unto him, saying, Thus shalt thou speak unto this people that spake unto thee, saying, Thy father made our yoke heavy, but make thou it lighter unto us; thus shalt thou say unto them, My little finger shall be thicker than my father's loins. 11 And now whereas my father did lade you with a heavy yoke, I will add to your yoke: my father hath chastised you with whips, but I will chastise you with scorpions."

After three days the people returned to Rehoboam,,,

13 "And the king answered the people roughly, and forsook the old men's counsel that they gave him; 14 And spake to them after the counsel of the young men, saying, My father made your yoke heavy, and I will add to your yoke: my father also chastised you with whips, but I will chastise you

with scorpions. 15 Wherefore the king hearkened not unto the people; for the cause was from the LORD, that he might perform his saying, which the LORD spake by Ahijah the Shilonite unto Jeroboam the son of Nebat."

As it turns out, Rehoboam was "right," in his own eyes. After all, he was the new king. However, even though he was right, he was not righteous. All the tribes of Israel separated themselves from Rehoboam and appointed a new king. Only the tribe of Judah stayed with Rehoboam. **Being right can be very costly**.

We have a classic New Testament case that illustrates this issue very well. [Matthew 26:31-35] In Matthew 26, we find Peter and the other disciples declaring their *rightness*. Jesus said they were not right but to no avail. The disciples had made up their minds and very strongly pronounced they were right. They were determined to be right no matter what anyone said to the contrary, including Jesus. They were right in their own eyes, no matter what the Scriptures said. However, they would find out later that they were not righteous in the eyes of God. In fact they were unrighteous, even as they strongly declared their *rightness*.

Matthew 26:35 "Peter said unto him, Though I should die with thee, yet will I not deny thee. Likewise also said all the disciples."

In verse 56, we find them scurrying and scattering.

No matter how loudly, definitely, and convincingly they shouted, they were still wrong. They had deceived themselves. This issue is as true for us as it was for them. The issue of *rightness* is greatly factored into man's decision making. If man has such a confidence in himself that no one can tell him he is wrong, he will make many wrong decisions based in his *rightness*. Henceforth he will make decisions according to *rightness*, not according to *righteousness*.

For the world at large, if they believe they are right, it matters not what the Word of God says. Most people do not consult the Bible for their standard of living; they consult themselves.

> Proverbs 16:2 "All the ways of a man are clean in his own eyes; but the LORD weigheth the spirits. 3 Commit thy works unto the LORD, and thy thoughts shall be established."

In addition to man's self-proclaimed *rightness*, there are decisions made according to preferences, pet peeves, political persuasions, and personal philosophies. All of these will complicate a person's ability to make good, sound, Biblical, righteous decisions. If you think chocolate is better than vanilla; that is simply your **opinion**.

To eat or not to eat that is the question!

> [Romans 14:1-23] 17 "For the kingdom of God is not meat and drink; but righteousness, and peace, and joy in the Holy Ghost."

> John 7:24 "Judge not according to the appearance, **but judge righteous judgment.**"

The danger in working so hard to prove you are right is that you might become unrighteous in the process and fail at love and kindness.

Matthew 26:9 "For this ointment might have been sold for much, and given to the poor."

Judas Iscariot was right. The ointment could have been sold, and then the proceeds could have been given to the poor. However, one thing is eternally true; Judas was not righteous. Even though the statement he made was true; his heart was dark and wicked. His desire was to be right in his own eyes; but he had NO desire to be righteous before God!

You can make a right or true statement and be unrighteous in how you say it. You might become unrighteous and cruel in the process of telling someone else how wrong they are. We must remember that life and death are in the power of the tongue. We can speak death words to someone who is wrong and be very unrighteous and wicked by telling them they are wrong.

"Pastor, you are not always right." As a pastor, I knew that was a true statement; but was the person making such a statement unrighteous in their observation?

The more mature spiritually a person becomes, the more it will become a matter of being righteous, not just *right*. The one who is spiritual will not fight the issues of preference, pet peeves, political persuasions, or personal philosophies, realizing there is no value in arguing or debating **in an interest to be *right***. The issue of being *right with God* will eclipse a person's desire to be *right in their own eyes* as they proclaim their own rightness to others. **Righteousness is about being right with God**. Righteousness is about God being right. The Bible say, "...let God be true, but **every man** a liar..."

Discernment & Decision Making

It is very important to learn the difference between rightness and righteousness. Many a pastor has run off church members over the issue of rightness, not righteousness. There are many church members who have left angry in their rightness and were very unrighteous and wicked to leave instead of making things right with others and with God as His Word tells us to do.

Righteousness has to do with being right with God, and to be right with God, we must be right with others or we will not be right with God.

> 1 John 4:20 "If a man say, I love God, and hateth his brother, he is a liar: for he that loveth not his brother whom he hath seen, how can he love God whom he hath not seen?"

There is many a father who has provoked his children to wrath over the issue of rightness, not righteousness. Do not be too bullheaded to know or learn the difference. Those under your care might not be right, but you must be righteous in the way you handle the issue, or both you and your child will fail the Father.

> James 1:19 "Wherefore, my beloved brethren, let every man be swift to hear, slow to speak, slow to wrath: 20 For **the wrath of man worketh not the righteousness of God.**"

The bottom line is that I must come to the conclusion that I am not right. You must come to the conclusion that you are not right. God is right, and the only way I can be righteous is in doing as Christ would do. God is right.

1 Kings 11:33 "Because that they have forsaken me, and have worshipped Ashtoreth the goddess of the Zidonians, Chemosh the god of the Moabites, and Milcom the god of the children of Ammon, and have not walked in my ways, to do **that which is right in mine eyes**, and *to keep* my statutes and my judgments, as *did* David his father. 38 And it shall be, if thou wilt hearken unto all that I command thee, and wilt walk in my ways, and do *that is* right in my sight, to keep my statutes and my commandments, as David my servant did; that I will be with thee, and build thee a sure house, as I built for David, and will give Israel unto thee."

We must remember that rightness is the number one contributing factor to all those in hell. Catholics, Muslims, Mormons, Mystics, Buddhists, Hindus, some Protestants, and some Baptists, and the like, will all be in hell over the issue of being right in their own eyes. People are less likely to go to hell believing they were wrong, than believing they were right. [Romans 10:1-4] There will not be a person in heaven who was right in their own eyes when it comes to the issue of salvation. When it comes to righteousness, God holds all the keys.

Do you want to be right or righteous? If you want to be righteous, then question your own rightness. If you do, you can and most likely will continue to seek and summit yourself to the righteousness of God. Rightness is not good enough. Righteousness pleases God, whereas rightness will only please you.

Love and Righteousness were mutilated, butchered, and brutalized at the cross as men chose rightness over Righteousness. Praise God, Jesus our Saviour and Righteous Redeemer chose to be there because He was and is Righteous. He prayed not for His own will but for the will of the Father to be done. He did always those things that pleased His Father. Even as He was upon the cross, He followed His own teachings to pray forgiveness for those who crucified Him. Love and Righteousness were mutilated, butchered, and brutalized at Calvary and not only did He survive, He triumphed. Righteousness rose from the dead to live. Righteousness always wins.

That is because rightness has temporal value whereas Righteousness has eternal value. Love and Righteousness have prevailed and will live forevermore.

1John 4:8 "He that loveth not knoweth not God; for **God is love**. 16 And we have known and believed the love that God hath to us. **God is love**; and he that dwelleth in love dwelleth in God, and God in him."

CHAPTER EIGHTEEN
You cannot give back your conscience

Matthew 27:1-5

[Matthew 26:1-5, 14, 15] Judas made a life changing decision, which he thought was for the betterment of his life. He forsook Christ, followed his own heart, leaned to his own understanding and walked away from the best thing he would ever know, because he never saw it as the best thing he would ever know. He believed there was more to life than following Jesus.

Judas had his ear to the world. He gave his heart to money. He was a man ruled by his own wicked desires. He made a deal with the Pharisees, not fully understanding what it would mean to his future. Just like Cain before him, after committing his crime, his punishment would turn out to be more than he could bear. His crime of blood would seal his fate.

The desire of his heart was supposed to bring him great happiness and sincere peace. The outcome was not at all what he had imagined. There is something he had not counted on when committing his crime against Christ.

[Matthew 27:1-5] The wheels of decision had moved forward with time and there was nothing Judas could have done to stop it once he led those evil men into the garden of Gethsemane. Judas' decision set eternal things in motion. After realizing he got something he really did not want, he tried to return his purchase, but to no avail.

Matthew 27:3 "Then Judas, which had betrayed him, when he saw that he was condemned, repented himself, and brought again the thirty pieces of silver to the chief priests and elders,"

Judas came back to the original scene of the crime, with the hope of giving back his sinful compensation. This was most likely done in an effort to return his responsibility in the crime that he and others had committed. He expected to hide and / or change the evidence against him.

He could not alter his responsibility or the outcome of it.

Matthew 27:4 "Saying, I have sinned in that I have betrayed the innocent blood. And they said, What is that to us? see thou to that."

He found his guilt was unbearable to live with. The blood money did not bring him the happiness he had diligently sought for. He took back the money, as if he wished to give back the guilt and shame he felt. It was not accepted any more than the thirty pieces of silver; both were forever his.

He found no sympathy from the cruel and heartless Pharisees. He found no place of refuge among the evil hate mongers. He found no hope and no peace from those devilish dogs.

He had been lied to by his own deceitful heart.

He found the money did not bring the happiness he had hoped for without spending a cent. He left the blood money on the floor of the temple, but he took his conscience with him after making his deal with the devil, and his friends.

John 12:6 "This he said, not that he cared for the poor; but because he was a thief, and had the bag, and bare what was put therein."

[Mathew 26:15—25] 15 "And said [unto them], What will ye give me, and I will deliver him unto you? And they covenanted with him for thirty pieces of silver." 25 Then Judas, which betrayed him, answered and said, Master, is it I? He said unto him, Thou hast said."

John 13: 2 "And supper being ended, the devil having now put into the heart of Judas Iscariot, Simon's son, to betray him; 27 And after the sop Satan entered into him. Then said Jesus unto him, That thou doest, do quickly."

Do not play with the devil or devilish things for they are not as harmless and attractive as they might at first appear to be. The hidden price is more expensive than the richest of men can afford to spend.

Ephesians 4:27 "Neither give place to the devil."

Ephesians 6:11 "Put on the whole armour of God, that ye may be able to stand against the wiles of the devil."

1 Timothy 3:6 "Not a novice, lest being lifted up with pride he fall into the condemnation of the devil. 7 Moreover he must have a good report of them which are without; lest he fall into reproach and the snare of the devil."

2 Timothy 2:26 "And [that] they may recover themselves out of the snare of the devil, who are taken captive by him at his will."

James 4:7 "Submit yourselves therefore to God. **Resist** the devil, and he will flee from you."

RESIST: oppose, withstand or stand against

Strong's Concordance

Instead of resisting or opposing the devil, Judas entertained and invited his influence, until Judas could not resist him even if he would have wanted to. When you play with the devil's fire, you will get burned. The devil was invited into the life of Judas to do his work.

Acts 7:51 "Ye stiffnecked and uncircumcised in heart and ears, ye do always **resist** the Holy Ghost: as your fathers *did*, so *do* ye."

RESIST: Oppose

Strong's Concordance

Judas resisted God, and God turned up the heat of Judas' conscience until it was completely seared from the application of "a hot iron."

1 Timothy 4:2 "Speaking lies in hypocrisy; having their conscience seared with a hot iron;"

Titus 1:15 "Unto the pure all things [are] pure: but unto them that are defiled and unbelieving [is] nothing pure; but even their mind and conscience is defiled."

2 Timothy 3:8 "Now as Jannes and Jambres withstood Moses, so do these also resist the truth: men of corrupt minds, reprobate concerning the faith."

When we do not resist, we are playing with fire.
Ephesians 4:17-24

Judas had not considered long or hard enough the consequence which should follow such a horrible decision. He would be haunted by his conscience. IT would bear the consequence of his greediness. IT would not let him escape. His conscience would torture him until he found no other solution but death. From there he would wake up in hell.

Mark 9:44 "Where their worm dieth not, and the fire is not quenched. 46 Where their worm dieth not, and the fire is not quenched. 48 Where their worm dieth not, and the fire is not quenched."

Luke 16:22 "And it came to pass, that the beggar died, and was carried by the angels into Abraham's bosom: the rich man also died, and was buried; 23 And in hell he lift up his eyes, being in torments, and seeth Abraham afar off, and Lazarus in his bosom. 24 And he cried and said, Father Abraham, have mercy on me, and send Lazarus, that he may dip the tip of his finger in water, and cool my tongue; for I am tormented in this flame. 25 But Abraham said, Son, remember that thou in thy lifetime receivedst thy good things, and likewise Lazarus evil things: but now he is comforted, and thou art tormented."

Discernment & Decision Making

Judas has an eternity to remember his mistake. Like the rich man before him, Judas found out the eternally hard way that money is not the solution, but a love for money is part of the problem. [Matthew 6:24]

> 1 Timothy 6:10 "For the love of money is the root of all evil: which while some coveted after, they have erred from the faith, and pierced themselves through with many sorrows. {erred: or, been seduced; Strong's Concordance}

> Matthew 27:5 "And he cast down the pieces of silver in the temple, and departed, and went and hanged himself."

Instead of spending his life **with** that money, he had spent his life **on** that money. The only lasting thing he was able to buy with HIS THIRY PIECES OF SILVER was an eternity of regret. His conscience will keep him company for eternity.

> Luke 16:25 "But Abraham said, Son, **remember** that thou in thy lifetime receivedst thy good things, and likewise Lazarus evil things: but now he is comforted, and thou art tormented."

> Matthew 26:24 "The Son of man goeth as it is written of him: but woe unto that man by whom the Son of man is betrayed! it had been good for that man if he had not been born."

You know what he probably thought? Would you like to guess what he came to realize or believe? The thought that drove him to get a rope and take it to a tree was the thought that "it had been good for that man if he had not been born." He came to believe he was better off

140

dead. He must have concluded that it would have been better, if he had never been born.

The anguish of his mind, the torture of his thoughts, and the agony of his guilt was absolutely unbearable.

Matthew 27:5 "And he cast down the pieces of silver in the temple, and departed, and went and hanged himself."

There was another time when the sound of money was heard hitting the temple floor.

Matthew 21:12 "And Jesus went into the temple of God, and cast out all them that sold and bought in the temple, and overthrew the tables of the moneychangers, and the seats of them that sold doves, 13 And said unto them, It is written, My house shall be called the house of prayer; but ye have made it a den of thieves."

The difference is, when Judas cast down the thirty pieces of silver onto the temple floor, there was a wicked, eerie, haunting, unholy, and unrighteous sound that echoed through eternity. When Jesus overturned the tables in the temple there was a righteous and a holy sound that rang throughout the temple, and forward in time.

What will be the report or recording of sounds you make in the church house? If your thoughts could be heard; would they be holy, or unholy? What sound does your conscience make? Judas' conscience made a very unholy sound, which became so unbearable he decided the only solution was to go and hang himself. He wanted to quiet his conscience so he decided it was better to die than to repent. However, repentance is more favorable than hell, I am sure.

CONSCIENCE, n. [L., to know, to be privy to.]

1. Internal or self-knowledge, or judgment of right and wrong; or the faculty, power or principle within us, which decides on the lawfulness or unlawfulness of our own actions and affections, and instantly approves or condemns them. Conscience is called by some writers the moral sense, and considered as an original faculty of our nature. Others question the propriety of considering conscience as a distinct faculty or principle. The consider it rather as the general principle of moral approbation or disapprobation, applied to ones own conduct and affections; alledging that our notions of right and wrong are not to be deduced from a single principle or faculty, but from various powers of the understanding and will.

Being convicted by their own conscience, they went out one by one. John 8.

The conscience manifests itself in the feeling of obligation we experience, which precedes, attends and follows our actions.

Conscience is first occupied in ascertaining our duty, before we proceed to action; then in judging of our actions when performed.

Noah Webster's 1828 Dictionary

CHAPTER NINETEEN
We must decide to have peace

Acts 10:1—48

Peter had great confidence regarding his rejection of the Gentiles. He was trained up to feel that way. Then while he was waiting for lunch to be served, he went into a trance. He was hungry, but not hungry enough to eat off the menu he was offered. He was so confident in his rejection he said, "Not so, Lord." The Lord worked to change Peter's mind and heart. After the sheet was let down and taken up the third time, Peter began to doubt in himself. He was not so secure in his decision to reject the Gentiles. He doubted in himself. Then there was a Gentile knock at the door. The Spirit told Peter to rise and go with the men "doubting nothing."

We can see that God nurtured the right response. If we are walking in the Spirit and we truly want to please God, and do His will, then He can and will nurture the truth in us, so that we can know and do the will of God.

There are many subjects, situations, and conditions a person will face in life that can cause great unrest and discontentment in their soul. Much of this unrest comes when our situation is at odds with our wants and desires. I have wondered about subjects such as a person who is deathly sick and thinking about eternity as the next major event on their calendar. I have thought about enduring the severe pain that accompanies disabilities, disease, or cancer where death is thought to be *a comfort in waiting*. I have considered a prisoner confined to bondage for the rest of their life because of bad choices they made. They know they will never be free again in this life. What is the thinking a person goes through, or the mindset they must have, in order to live in these types of serious conditions?

We certainly must learn to accept what we cannot change.

Peace is something that everyone wants. There are many things that man can do without, but to do without peace is the most agonizing and excruciating way to exist. Peace will help a man survive any condition of life. Peace can be achieved by accepting the things we cannot change; that might be easier said than done. It is a way of coming to terms with difficult situations.

You can be poor or rich and be without peace. You can be in prison or living in the most beautiful palace of plenty and have no peace. You can be deathly sick in bed or be the fittest of athletes and be without peace. Peace is a matter of the soul, not necessarily an external condition of circumstance. A person can have peace even during a bad situation because they make right decisions in the midst of bad circumstances.

The peace of Christ will take us beyond any difficult circumstance. **It will allow us to soar with the eagles in triumphant even as we are buried beneath a mountain of troubles. It will allow us to march boldly as a lion in a parade of gazelles, even when we are the gazelle, in the lion's parade**. The peace that comes from God the Holy Spirit can give us the heart of victory even when we lie dying in our own blood.

> Acts 7:59 "And they stoned Stephen, calling upon God, and saying, Lord Jesus, receive my spirit. 60 And he kneeled down, and cried with a loud voice, Lord, lay not this sin to their charge. And when he had said this, he fell asleep."

Unfortunately, not everyone knows how to have lasting peace. This is because most men rely on their own understanding to bring themselves peace. Truthfully, peace comes from making right decisions. A wrong decision can put you in a bad situation, whereas a good decision will make your circumstance good.

Godly peace comes by making godly decisions. Peace comes from living righteous and / or as a result of making righteous decisions. Righteous decisions are decisions made when we converse with God in prayer, and as we consult God's Word, and as we seek God's will.

We need the peace of God as we face discouragement.

1 Samuel 30:6 "And David was greatly distressed; for the people spake of stoning him, because the soul of all the people was grieved, every man for his sons and for his daughters: but David encouraged himself in the LORD his God. 7 And David said to Abiathar the priest, Ahimelech's son, I pray thee, bring me hither the ephod. And Abiathar brought thither the ephod to David. 8 And David enquired at the LORD, saying, Shall I pursue after this troop? shall I overtake them? And he answered him, Pursue: for thou shalt surely overtake them, and without fail recover all."

David was faced with discouraged people who were trying to cope with a frustrating situation. Instead of being discouraged by these people, David chose to be encouraged and influenced by God in his decision making. After going to God for consultation, David took God's advice, fought the Amalekites, and was able to win and recuperate everything that was thought to be lost because he followed the Word of God. Not only did they recover the people and possessions, they also recovered peace because David made the right decision.

> 2 Samuel 2:1 "And it came to pass after this, that David enquired of the LORD, saying, Shall I go up into any of the cities of Judah? And the LORD said unto him, Go up. And David said, Whither shall I go up? And he said, Unto Hebron."

> 2 Samuel 5:19 "And David enquired of the LORD, saying, Shall I go up to the Philistines? wilt thou deliver them into mine hand? And the LORD said unto David, Go up: for I will doubtless deliver the Philistines into thine hand."

When consulting God while making a decision, you will get peace by receiving affirmation from Him. No matter what happens after the decision is made, if the decision is made in consultation with God, and God tells you what to do, and you do what He says to do, the outcome is in God's hands.

Israel faced a time when they had joined together in response to an evil which had been committed in Benjamin. Israel consulted with God. God told them to go against Benjamin.

[Judges 20:1—48] In Judges 20, Israel faced a horrible situation. They were challenged to make a decision whereby they would face their own brothers in battle. They had tried to settle the matter by simply dealing with those who committed a grievous offense. Benjamin refused Israel's terms for peace. In Judges 20, 18, 23, we find Israel "asked counsel of the LORD" and the LORD told them to go against Benjamin. Both times they failed. They had consulted with God, He told them to go up, they did and yet they failed to defeat Benjamin in battle.

> Judges 20: 27 "And the children of Israel enquired of the LORD, (for the ark of the covenant of God was there in those days, 28 And Phinehas, the son of Eleazar, the son of Aaron, stood before it in those days,) saying, Shall I yet again go out to battle against the children of Benjamin my brother, or shall I cease? And the LORD said, Go up; for to morrow I will deliver them into thine hand."

Before going into battle the third time, Israel fasted, prayed, and asked God for counsel, again. The third time was the first time God told them they would win. Certainly during the first two failures it would have been easy for Israel, and Benjamin, to misdiagnose the conclusion. We must gain understanding from this story. Just because there will be setbacks does not necessarily mean God is not in the decision you made in consultation with God.

In fact, it is likely that when Benjamin gained advantage during the first two battles, they might have gained a false peace and security from their perceived victory. When things seem to go our way it does not mean God is with us and when things do not necessarily go our way, it does not mean God is not with us. [Exodus 14] Things can change very quickly with the parting of the Red Sea of trouble. We must be careful not to assume or draw conclusions too quickly. The verdict is still out until God has spoken.

> Exodus 14:10 "And when Pharaoh drew nigh, the children of Israel lifted up their eyes, and, behold, the Egyptians marched after them; and they were sore afraid: and the children of Israel cried out unto

the LORD. 11 And they said unto Moses, Because there were no graves in Egypt, hast thou taken us away to die in the wilderness? wherefore hast thou dealt thus with us, to carry us forth out of Egypt? 12 Is not this the word that we did tell thee in Egypt, saying, Let us alone, that we may serve the Egyptians? For it had been better for us to serve the Egyptians, than that we should die in the wilderness. 13 And Moses said unto the people, Fear ye not, stand still, and see the salvation of the LORD, which he will shew to you to day: for the Egyptians whom ye have seen to day, ye shall see them again no more for ever."

Moses had peace even though the children of Israel did not. Moses knew he was where God wanted him, and he knew he was there at the right time. Moses was in-tune with God; the people and Pharaoh were not.

Exodus 14: 1 "And the LORD spake unto Moses, saying, 2 Speak unto the children of Israel, that they turn and encamp before Pihahiroth, between Migdol and the sea, over against Baalzephon: before it shall ye encamp by the sea. 3 For Pharaoh will say of the children of Israel, They are entangled in the land, the wilderness hath shut them in. 4 And I will harden Pharaoh's heart, that he shall follow after them; and I will be honoured upon Pharaoh, and upon all his host; that the Egyptians may know that I am the LORD. And they did so."

Noah lived in peace for 100 years while building an ark, because he made the decision to do what God said. Abraham could go to the top of the mountain to sacrifice his only son because he made a decision to obey God. He did what, where, when, and how he was told to offer his son. He made his decision in peace and staggered not at the promises of God. Abraham certainly had a peace that passes ALL understanding, in order to agree to do what God required of him. He was able to set aside his doubt and fear and do the unthinkable. God gave him an incredibly amount of graceful peace.

Daniel went to prayer in peace as it was his habit to do, even though he knew a decree had been written against making a petition to his God. He feared not the lion's den because peace resided in his heart. The three Hebrews agreed to Nebuchadnezzar's fire, refusing to bow down to the golden image because they had the peace that passes understanding down in their hearts.

David fought Goliath in peace. Jonathan fought the Philistines in peace. Hezekiah was able to lay out the letter from Sennacherib, king of Assyria, before God, and rise up in peace. Hezekiah told God that He had a problem. Elisha faced the Syrians with his spiritual eyes opened. He had great peace because he trusted God, and put no faith in the armies of the enemy. He wore the armor of God daily.

> 2 Kings 6: 16 "And he answered, Fear not: for they that be with us are more than they that be with them. 17 And Elisha prayed, and said, LORD, I pray thee, open his eyes, that he may see. And the LORD opened the eyes of the young man; and he saw: and, behold, the mountain was full of horses and chariots of fire round about Elisha."

Men like Noah, Abraham, Moses, David, Daniel, The Three Hebrews, Elijah, Elisha, Stephen, and Paul lived their life by making decisions that pleased God. They made decisions to follow God and then swore to their own hurt.

> Psalm 15:4 "In whose eyes a vile person is contemned; but he honoureth them that fear the LORD. He that sweareth to his own hurt, and changeth not."

> Ecclesiastes 5:4 "When thou vowest a vow unto God, defer not to pay it; for [he hath] no pleasure in fools: pay that which thou hast vowed. 5 Better [is it] that thou shouldest not vow, than that thou shouldest vow and not pay."

There will always be room for the devil to work *after* a decision, as well as *before* it is made. It has been said that *we must not undo in doubt the decision we have made in faith*. The decision we make must be the decision we keep when it is of God. Once we believe we have made a decision that is in accordance with the will of God, we must swear to our own hurt.

The peace of Christ will take us beyond any difficult circumstance. It will allow us to soar with the eagles in triumphant even as we are buried beneath a mountain of troubles. It will allow us to march boldly as a lion in a parade of gazelles, even when we are the gazelle, in the lion's parade. The peace that comes from God the Holy Spirit can give us the heart of victory even when we lie dying in our own blood.

> Psalms 15:4 "In whose eyes a vile person is contemned; but he honoureth them that fear the LORD. *He that* sweareth to *his own* hurt, and changeth not."

Jesus went to God and asked for His Father to remove the cup of sin from Him. There was no response offered to Jesus' prayer. He knew what He had to do. He went to the cross without protest because He knew He was doing the will of God. That does not mean He did not feel the heavy burden and anguish before His decision. It does show us there can be heaviness in heart before we come to peace that we made the right decision. Jesus made a decision, and then swore to His own hurt.

> Philippians 4:7 "And the peace of God, which passeth all understanding, shall keep your hearts and minds through Christ Jesus."

> Colossians 3:15 "And let the peace of God rule in your hearts, to the which also ye are called in one body; and be ye thankful."

The peace of God works like an umpire calling balls and strikes. A pitcher throws a pitch to the catcher at home plate. The umpire decides whether it is a strike or a ball. When we throw a decision to God for review like a pitcher throws a pitch, God the Holy Spirit will let us know if we are throwing a strike or a ball. As we walk in the Spirit, in tune with the Holy Spirit, doing God's will, he will give us peace. However, if we are doing our own will, outside the strike zone, we will be troubled without God's peace.

We can stand against fire, fruitlessness, lions, giants, and the armies of the enemy with great peace as we stand firm in the will of God. There is no peace, only troubling waters in the heart, when God is not in, or with, what we are doing.

There is a clear Biblical picture that illustrates being troubled by a decision a person has made. It is found in 1 Samuel 24. Saul was pursuing David to kill him. He went up into the mountains chasing David. In the process, Saul went into a cave to rest. It just happened to be the cave that contained David and his men. His men suggested that the LORD had delivered Saul into David's hand so he could kill him. David must have wrestled with such a decision.

> 1 Samuel 24:4 "And the men of David said unto him, Behold the day of which the LORD said unto thee, Behold, I will deliver thine enemy into thine hand, that thou mayest do to him as it shall seem good unto thee. Then David arose, and cut off the skirt of Saul's robe privily. 5 And it came to pass afterward, that David's heart smote him, because he had cut off Saul's skirt."

Instead of killing Saul, David cut his skirt. It seems that David might have been testing the waters to check the temperature of such a major decision. The simple and seemingly harmless act was wrong enough for God to smite David's heart. He got David's attention by smiting his heart, and turned him away from any thoughts he might have entertained about killing Saul. If he had killed Saul he would have been guilty of touching the Lord's anointed.

> 1 Chronicles 16:22 "Saying, Touch not mine anointed, and do my prophets no harm."

> Psalms 105:15 "Saying, Touch not mine anointed, and do my prophets no harm."

Discernment & Decision Making

By smiting David's heart, while he was in the process of putting a knife to the garment of God's anointed king, God let David know he was too close to danger. He needed to *cease and desist* from the decision that certainly had gone through David's mind.

> 1 Samuel 24: 6 "And he said unto his men, The LORD forbid that I should do this thing unto my master, the LORD'S anointed, to stretch forth mine hand against him, seeing he is the anointed of the LORD. 7 So David stayed his servants with these words, and suffered them not to rise against Saul. But Saul rose up out of the cave, and went on his way. 8 David also arose afterward, and went out of the cave, and cried after Saul, saying, My lord the king. And when Saul looked behind him, David stooped with his face to the earth, and bowed himself."

God can trouble our heart or give us peace as a way to direct us. If we are seeking God's will, we can know it as God directs our heart. Yes, the heart can deceive us, and yet even then, God can allow it to be so for His will to be done. He can deal with us as we seek a direction in opposition to the will of God. We see this in Balaam's life.

[Numbers 22: 15-22] Balaam sought to curse the children of Israel at the request of Balak. God had told Balaam, "No." However, since Balaam was seeking his own will and not God's, God allowed him to pursue an agenda He would never bless. God angrily let Balaam go with the men from Moab.

In Numbers 11, we find that God had said, "No" to the children of Israel, and then gave them quail up to their necks. He then judged these rebellious people. He gave them what they wanted to turn them from their way and cultivate a desire for the will of God in them.

> Numbers 11:31 "And there went forth a wind from the LORD, and brought quails from the sea, and let them fall by the camp, as it were a day's journey on this side, and as it were a day's journey on the other side, round about the camp, and as it were two cubits high upon the face of the earth. 32 And the people stood up all that day, and all that night, and all the next day, and they gathered the quails: he that gathered least gathered ten homers: and they spread them all abroad for themselves round about the camp. 33 And while the flesh was yet between their teeth, ere it was chewed, the wrath of the LORD was kindled against the people, and the LORD smote the people with a very great plague. 34 And he called the name of that place Kibrothhattaavah: because there they buried the people that lusted.

> {Kibrothhattaavah: that is, The **graves of lust**}

> *Strong's Concordance*

How many graves of lust are in your life and mine? These would be graves of buried decisions where we *leaned* to and *lusted* after our own understanding. This would be times when God allowed us to have our way so that we might better realize the hard way so that we should desire His way.

Oh, how often God works to caution us from going the wrong way! How He troubles our heart about wrong decisions! He is ever working to cultivate a desire in us for the ways of God. He gives attention, shows interest, and oversees every move we make. As a Father with His children, God is at work with every decision we make.

> Proverbs 5:21 "For the ways of man are before the eyes of the LORD, and he pondereth all his goings."

> Proverbs 16:9 "A man's heart deviseth his way: but the LORD directeth his steps."

As we start taking steps in His direction, we will have peace that increases with each step we take, even in the midst of conflict. His peace will not come as we sit and wait, but as we move in the right direction. As we devise a way, He will direct our steps. At the beginning, we will not know all the details, but we can know His peace.

God might give us peace about a decision, but there will still be a little doubt in the details. This is where faith comes into play. Faith will always be a part of our decision making. We will not know everything when we make a decision, for without faith, it is impossible to please God.

Not knowing all the details keeps many people from committing to a decision they believe God wants them to make. The danger is in not making a decision, or trying to embrace two directions at the same time. We must make a decision by devising a way, which we believe is God's will, and then allow the Lord to direct our steps.

> James 1:8 "A double minded man [is] unstable in all his ways."

As we read our Bible, faithfully pray, walk in the Spirit, obey God, seek His will, and acknowledge Him with every decision we make, God will give us peace in our decision making. He will direct our path. As we decide to follow God, we will enjoy His peace.

The peace that comes from Christ takes us beyond any difficult circumstance. It will allow us to soar with the eagles in triumph even as we are buried beneath a mountain of troubles. It will allow us to march boldly as a lion in a parade of gazelles, even when we are the gazelle, in the lion's parade. The peace that comes from God the Holy Spirit can give us the heart of victory even when we lie dying in our own blood.

Acts 7:59 "And they stoned Stephen, calling upon God, and saying, Lord Jesus, receive my spirit. 60 And he kneeled down, and cried with a loud voice, Lord, lay not this sin to their charge. And when he had said this, he fell asleep."

CHAPTER TWENTY
Not early or late, but right on time

1 Corinthians 7: 1 "Now concerning the things whereof ye wrote unto me: It is good for a man not to touch a woman. 2 Nevertheless, *to avoid* fornication, let every man have his own wife, and let every woman have her own husband."

The relations and pleasures that a husband and wife are able to enjoy is right in the eyes of the Lord, when conducted inside the bounds of marriage. Yet when a man and woman are joined together outside of marriage, they are committing fornication. **It is a matter of doing the right thing at the right time verses the right thing at the wrong time**. If a man touches a woman outside the marriage vows, he commits fornication. When he touches a woman inside of marriage, the bed of marriage is undefiled.

Hebrews 13:4 "Marriage *is* honourable in all, and the bed undefiled: but whoremongers and adulterers God will judge."

When making a decision we must consider timing. It is not just a matter of the right decision, but the timing must be right as well.

[Matthew 4:1—11] The devil came to tempt Jesus three times at one setting. One of the ways he tempted Jesus was with the kingdoms of the world and the glory of them.

Matthew 4:8 "Again, the devil taketh him up into an exceeding high mountain, and sheweth him all the kingdoms of the world, and the glory of them; 9 And saith unto him, All these things will I give thee, if thou wilt fall down and worship me."

The devil presently has ownership of the world's kingdoms. He promised to transfer ownership to Jesus, *if* He would bow down and worship him. Jesus gave the devil an eternal, Holy Scripture response and sent him packing.

Matthew 4:10 "Then saith Jesus unto him, Get thee hence, Satan: for it is written, Thou shalt worship the Lord thy God, and him only shalt thou serve."

Satan's presentation to Jesus was the right thing for Jesus, but it was offered at the wrong time. One day everyone will worship Jesus. All glory will eventually be His forever. Yet first, Jesus had to go to the cross, die, and rise again to conquer and receive the kingdoms Satan had subtly offered.

Philippians 2: 9 "Wherefore God also hath highly exalted him, and given him a name which is above every name: 10 That at the name of Jesus every knee should bow, of things in heaven, and things in earth, and things under the earth; 11 And that every tongue should confess that Jesus Christ is Lord, to the glory of God the Father."

The glory of this world's kingdoms might have seemed like they were offered at a bargain price, but they were not. It might have seemed like a way to get glory without the death of the cross; but it was not. [John 12:23-25]

Philippians 2:5 "Let this mind be in you, which was also in Christ Jesus: 6 Who, being in the form of God, thought it not robbery to be equal with God: 7

But made himself of no reputation, and took upon him the form of a servant, and was made in the likeness of men: 8 And being found in fashion as a man, he humbled himself, and became obedient unto death, even the death of the cross."

When making decisions, it is not good enough to make the right decision. Decisions must be made at the right time. Decisions that are made at the wrong time will be filled with corruption.

We can also take comfort in knowing that God is Sovereign. He is in control of all things. He never takes time off. He is ever vigilant and diligently working behind the scenes to accomplish His will.

Proverbs 16:9 "A man's heart deviseth his way: but the LORD directeth his steps."

As man is in tune with God, devising a way to accomplish the will of God, he can take comfort in knowing that God will ever be working to direct his steps. As we acknowledge God with every decision we make, we can take comfort in knowing He has already been working to direct our steps, before we decided to do His will.

Consider the story of Cornelius and Peter from Acts 10. These two men were both seeking the will and way of God. They did not know each other; but their lives intersect because God was directing them both. In this story you can see the amazing timing of God.

At the beginning of the chapter, we find Cornelius, a man who obviously desired to be right with God. God responds in a wonderful and unusual way to Cornelius' prayers. He sent an angel to tell Cornelius of Caesarea, to send men to fetch Peter from Simon the tanner's house, who lived in Joppa.

The next day they went. On that day, Peter got hungry and decided to go to the housetop while lunch was being made and fell into a trance. While in this state, a sheet-like vessel was let down from heaven with an uncommon assortment of food. He was told to rise and eat. At first considering this might be some kind of test, he replied confidently, "Not so, Lord." After this is done the third time, Peter "doubted in himself." He then woke from the trance, pondering the meaning of this strange vision. As he did, The Holy Spirit told Peter that three men sought him.

Sure enough, at that moment, there were three Gentiles, sent by Cornelius to Peter, knocking at the gate. The Holy Spirit told Peter he was to arise and go with these Gentiles, "doubting nothing", because they were sent by Him.

God the Holy Spirit was working out the timing at each step. From the time Cornelius saw the angel, till the time Peter agreed to go with these men, was less than twenty-four hours. They lodged there that night and left from Joppa to Caesarea the next day. From start to finish it took a total of four days from the angel's visit to Cornelius till Peter arrived in Caesarea. When Peter arrived, many of those who had gathered with Cornelius were gloriously saved.

At the end of Acts chapter 10, you could conclude that this event was the beginning of the acceptance and institution of the gospel ministry to the Gentiles.

Acts 9:15 "But the Lord said unto him, Go thy way: for he is a chosen vessel unto me, to bear my name before the Gentiles, and kings, and the children of Israel: 16 For I will shew him how great things he must suffer for my name's sake."

Even before Cornelius and Peter intersected, God saved a man named Saul in Acts 9. Saul was the man who would become Paul. Paul is the man who was given responsibility of the Gentile ministry after God established it in Acts 10. This is all part of God's timing.

In chapter 11, we find the apostles and brethren questioned Peter about consorting with the Gentiles. Peter explained to these Jews about the sign of God's working among the Gentiles. They accepted that this new Gentile ministry was of God. They could not deny the timing of God.

Acts 13: 1 "Now there were in the church that was at Antioch certain prophets and teachers; as Barnabas, and Simeon that was called Niger, and Lucius of Cyrene, and Manaen, which had been brought up with Herod the tetrarch, and Saul. 2 As they ministered to the Lord, and fasted, the Holy Ghost said, Separate me Barnabas and Saul for the work whereunto I have called them. 3 And when they had fasted and prayed, and laid their hands on them, they sent them away."

God's timing is everything

NOTES TO LIVE BY: Note to self, ask GOD for wisdom and discernment every day.

Make sure all my plans are Biblically based, spiritually "well-watered," and bathed in prayer, so that I keep Christ and eternity in focus.

If I favor God, then God will favor me: Deuteronomy 30:15-21. Obeying God will ensure a blessed life.

I need to have long term thinking in my decision making. I must not have knot-hole philosophy.

Bad decisions will ripple through my life, so I must be careful not to make decisions I will regret.

Ask God to help me see the dangerous in what appears to be tame. I must put on the whole armor or God, daily.

The Word of God will not work in my life unless I apply it, every day.

MEMORIZE: Romans 15:4 "For whatsoever things were written aforetime were written for our learning, that we through patience and comfort of the scriptures might have hope."

I must make sure my decisions are righteous, not just right.

CHAPTER TWENTY-ONE
The fear of the LORD is the beginning

Psalms 25: 4 "Shew me thy ways, O LORD; teach me thy paths. 5 Lead me in thy truth, and teach me: for thou art the God of my salvation; on thee do I wait all the day. 12 What man is he that feareth the LORD? him shall he teach in the way that he shall choose. 13 His soul shall dwell at ease; and his seed shall inherit the earth. 14 The secret of the LORD is with them that fear him; and he will shew them his covenant."

As you study the Word of God, you will find that the fear of the LORD is the answer to decision making. The LORD will teach and show His ways unto those who fear Him. The secret of the LORD is with those who fear Him.

Proverbs 2: 1 "My son, if thou wilt receive my words, and hide my commandments with thee; 2 So that thou incline thine ear unto wisdom, and apply thine heart to understanding; 3 Yea, if thou criest after knowledge, and liftest up thy voice for understanding; 4 If thou seekest her as silver, and searchest for her as for hid treasures; 5 **Then** shalt thou understand the fear of the LORD, and find the knowledge of God."

The best decision makers are those who listen to wisdom, seek understanding, and cry for knowledge as if it were a hidden and valuable treasure. Those who do will understand the fear of God. Then they will find knowledge.

Proverbs 29:25 "The fear of man bringeth a snare: but whoso putteth his trust in the LORD shall be safe."

163

Proverbs 28:5 "Evil men understand not judgment: but they that seek the LORD understand all things."

To fear the LORD is to have a desire to please Him above all others, above all things. Pleasing God is the beginning and end of a peaceful life.

Proverbs 9:10 "The fear of the LORD *is* the beginning of wisdom: and the knowledge of the holy *is* understanding."

Proverbs 14:26 "In the fear of the LORD *is* strong confidence: and his children shall have a place of refuge."

Proverbs 14:27 "The fear of the LORD *is* a fountain of life, to depart from the snares of death."

Proverbs 15:16 "Better *is* little with the fear of the LORD than great treasure and trouble therewith."

Proverbs 19:23 "The fear of the LORD *tendeth* to life: and *he that hath it* shall abide satisfied; he shall not be visited with evil."

Proverbs 22:4 "By humility *and* the fear of the LORD *are* riches, and honour, and life."

Decisions will be more easily made if we fear God. If we refuse to fear God, we will complicate our life.

CHAPTER TWENTY-TWO
Wrong decisions were made to be changed

When we discover we have made a wrong decision, we must have courage to change our mind and right the wrong. We can reverse our wrong direction and make it right. There might be consequences we have to suffer as we reap what we have sown, but God can give us grace as we have courage to turn from our wrong decisions and go back the other way. Usually it is pride that keeps us from admitting our wrongs.

Herod kept his oath, but John the Baptist lost his head.

[Mark 6:17—29] King Herod made an oath to give away half his kingdom because he delighted in the dance of a young damsel. After consulting with her mother, she decided she did not want half the kingdom; she wanted the head of John the Baptist. This was done at a very public birthday party. There were many prestigious spectators who heard the king's oath and her request. Herod must have felt trapped. He consented to do what he really did not have the heart to do. Since pride ruled his heart, he agreed to give the girl the head of John the Baptist, to save face. He knew he was agreeing to kill a man he believed was just to keep an unjust promise to save his own name. He made a wicked promise he should never have made; he kept a promise he should have broken.

Jeremiah, "Thou speakest falsely..."

If you read Jeremiah 40—43, you will find the children of Israel were faced with what they thought was a difficult decision. The question for them was whether they should stay or go. Should they stay in Jerusalem or flee to Egypt. They believed that if they should stay, the king of

Babylon would come to kill them once he found out that evil men had killed the governor that the king of Babylon had put in charge.

They went to seek counsel from the man of God about what they should do. Jeremiah went to get them counsel from God as they gave their word promising, they would do whatever God said to do. God told Jeremiah to tell them to stay, and they would be safe. However, if they fled to Egypt they would die. This seemed unreasonable to them. It went against the direction they had already decided to go. They had made a commitment by their actions. **Then** they went to ask Jeremiah to seek God's counsel.

> Jeremiah 41:17 "And they departed, and dwelt in the habitation of Chimham, which is by Bethlehem, **to go to enter into Egypt**, 18 Because of the Chaldeans: for they were afraid of them, because Ishmael the son of Nethaniah had slain Gedaliah the son of Ahikam, whom the king of Babylon made governor in the land." Jeremiah 42:1 "**Then** all the captains of the forces, and Johanan the son of Kareah, and Jezaniah the son of Hoshaiah, and all the people from the least even unto the greatest, came near, 2 And said unto Jeremiah the prophet, Let, we beseech thee, our supplication be accepted before thee, and pray for us unto the LORD thy God, even for all this remnant; (for we are left but a few of many, as thine eyes do behold us:) 3 That the LORD thy God may shew us the way wherein we may walk, and the thing that we may do."

Jeremiah returned from consulting with the LORD and told them if they stayed they would live and if they fled to Egypt they would die. They told Jeremiah, "Thou speakest falsely..."

> Jeremiah 43: 1 "And it came to pass, that when Jeremiah had made an end of speaking unto all the people all the words of the LORD their God, for which the LORD their God had sent him to them, even all these words, 2 Then spake Azariah the son of Hoshaiah, and Johanan the son of Kareah, and all the proud men, saying unto Jeremiah, Thou speakest falsely: the LORD our God hath not sent thee to say, Go not into Egypt to sojourn there: 3 But Baruch the son of Neriah setteth thee on against us, for to deliver us into the hand of the Chaldeans, that they might put us to death, and carry us away captives into Babylon. 4 So Johanan the son of Kareah, and all the captains of the forces, and all the people, obeyed not the voice of the LORD, to dwell in the land of Judah."

They felt they could not change the physical direction they had already set their heart to travel. Notice in verse 2, it is "proud men" that keep them on the wrong course. Because they were right in their own eyes instead of righteous, they died in sin. They rejected the word they promised to obey. God instructed them to follow His path of life, but they choose a path of death [Deuteronomy 30:15-20]. Not only do we need spiritual wisdom to make righteous decisions, we also need spiritual character, courage, and humility to undo wrong decisions.

Pilate went against his BETTER judgment.

Mark 15:9 "But Pilate answered them, saying, Will ye that I release unto you the King of the Jews? 10

For he knew that the chief priests had delivered him for envy. 11 But the chief priests moved the people, that he should rather release Barabbas unto them. 12 And Pilate answered and said again unto them, What will ye then that I shall do unto him whom ye call the King of the Jews? 13 And they cried out again, Crucify him. 14 Then Pilate said unto them, Why, what evil hath he done? And they cried out the more exceedingly, Crucify him. 15 And so Pilate, **willing to content the people**, released Barabbas unto them, and delivered Jesus, when he had scourged him, to be crucified."

[Matthew 27:11—25; Luke 23:1—25; John 19:1—13]

Pilate knew it was wrong. He knew they were envious of Jesus. He examined Jesus to look for the wrong the Pharisees said was there. He found NO fault in Jesus. Pilate's conclusion was that Jesus was innocent. He tried to convince the vicious mob to let Jesus go. They refused any condition other than crucifixion. They hated Jesus. So in order to keep favor with the people, Pilate sentenced an innocent man to be crucified. He did what he knew was wrong in an effort to please the people.

There is a difference between a commitment and a decision. A commitment, such as marriage, cannot be broken [Ecclesiastes 5:4]. However, a decision, like not tithing, or taking a wrong job, can be broken. There are many such decisions people make which they refuse to forsake when they are ruled by their pride. Keep Godly commitments, but abandon wrong decisions and seek the grace of God to be right with Him.

How wrong is the decision that you intend to keep?

A SUMMARY of additional thoughts

[Acts 6:1—15] Good leaders should surround themselves with other good leaders. Moses chose choice men to judge the people. Stephen and the others were chosen out of the crowd to manage an important duty because of their wisdom, and the spiritual walk they maintained. Spiritual people are profitable because spiritual people make spiritual decisions. Stephen was a student of God and walked in the Spirit. Therefore he was chosen by the leadership to be a leader in the church.

Good leaders will want to surround themselves with spiritual people who have an understanding of the Word of God, and knowledge of its principles. These types of people will usually walk in the Spirit throughout the day. They are profitable because they do not have to be baby-sat. They are mature, and they are prone to make mature decisions. In addition to not causing more stress, they actually help to alleviate stress others have caused. They do not stress the body but help to stabilize it. They will work to maintain unity with others. This unity will mean there will be fewer decisions to make.

There are many more stories in the Bible that could and should be sited so that we might learn from the ensamples of those God gave us to learn from. We must be students of the Bible if we hope to make good and righteous decisions.

The following comments are additional thoughts which I felt had a place in this book. However, I did not feel led to devote a chapter to each thought, but rather **decided** a line or two would be best.

Discernment & Decision Making

That brings me to the first thought. When making decisions we must consider what is best, not just what is better. Never assume facts not in evidence. Assumptions will most often take you in a wrong direction during decision making. You should not decide based merely on past experience [John 7:24]. Be sure to apply the Word equally to all sides of the issue, not just to satisfy personal preferences and feelings.

Testimony does matter when considering conversation. Is the person you are consulting or conversing with trustworthy? Is the Word of God or the principles of God's word being violated to achieve a desired end? If the Word of God will be compromised, it is best not to make such a decision. Remember, some people will compromise and call it peace.

Communication is very important. No matter if you are in charge, or you are consulting with your authority, be a good listener either way. You might learn more than you already know. Every situation is different, even when it might look the same. Be a good student, even if you are the teacher.

James 1:19 "Wherefore, my beloved brethren, let every man be swift to hear, slow to speak, slow to wrath:"

Ecclesiastes 5:1 "Keep thy foot when thou goest to the house of God, and be more ready to hear, than to give the sacrifice of fools: for they consider not that they do evil. 2 Be not rash with thy mouth, and let not thine heart be hasty to utter any thing before God: for God is in heaven, and thou upon earth: therefore let thy words be few. 3 For a dream

170

cometh through the multitude of business; and a fool's voice is known by multitude of words."

Pray over every decision. Do not make hasty decisions. Try to always wait a day or more; to allow God time to speak to you or those you are in a decision with. {I had someone tell me once they wait three days, a day for each person of the Trinity.} Waiting will give God the opportunity to veto the decision you are considering. This extra time will also give God time to fix you.

Make sure you leave yourself plenty of room to be wrong. Pride is an ugly thing. When you build walls of pride, you can become trapped with no way out. You might get to the place where you will not be able to say you were wrong. That is an island you do not want to live on. It only looks attractive and serene on a post card.

Do not go to an unjust person or judge for judgment [1 Corinthians 6:1-11]. Remember the measurement of judgment you use will be the yard stick God uses to judge you. That truth is to be a guide as a measurement of mercy as we make decisions [Matthew 7:1, 2]. Jesus said we are not to judge by appearance only, but we are to judge by righteous judgment [John 7:24]

Walk in the Spirit every day. Do not grieve or quench the Holy Spirit in your life. You will not be a good decision maker if you are a griever or quencher of the Spirit.

John 14:26 "But the Comforter, *which is* the Holy Ghost, whom the Father will send in my name, he shall teach you all things, and bring all things to your remembrance, whatsoever I have said unto you."

Discernment & Decision Making

Make sure to maintain a good working relationship with the Word of God. We must read and study the Bible daily so that it is always part of our thought process. **If you get away from the Bible for any amount of time, then you have already made a bad decision**. More will likely follow.

> Hebrews 4:12 "For the word of God is quick, and powerful, and sharper than any twoedged sword, piercing even to the dividing asunder of soul and spirit, and of the joints and marrow, and is a discerner of the thoughts and intents of the heart."

Solomon got his wisdom to discern from the LORD.

> 1 Kings 3:24 "And the king said, **Bring me a sword**. And they brought a sword before the king. 25 And the king said, Divide the living child in two, and give half to the one, and half to the other. 26 Then spake the woman whose the living child was unto the king, for her bowels yearned upon her son, and she said, O my lord, give her the living child, and in no wise slay it. But the other said, Let it be neither mine nor thine, but divide it. 27 Then the king answered and said, Give her the living child, and in no wise slay it: she is the mother thereof. 28 And all Israel heard of the judgment which the king had judged; and they feared the king: for they saw that the wisdom of God was in him, to do judgment."

Books by this author:

Authority

Thou art the man

Discernment & Decision Making